Justin Taylor grew up on a sugar farm in Zululand and spoke Zulu before he could speak English. He was sent to boarding school for ten years before reporting for National Service in 1979. Doing 'your bit' for your country ran in Taylor's family - his grandfather was a fighter pilot in the Royal Flying Corps and in the Second World War his father flew Spitfires for the SAAF.

In 1979 he was drafted into the military, completing two years of National Service, including serving as a Signals Officer with 32 Battalion in the Namibian/Angolan conflict (1979-80). Justin was wounded at the Battle of Savate and awarded the Chief of SADF Commendation Medal (MMM, or Military Merit Medal as it was later renamed) for services of a high order. He then went on to complete part-time military service with 2 Reconnaissance Regiment.

Justin holds a BA from the University of Cape Town, majoring in Economics and Psychology and a Masters Degree (MBL) from the University of South Africa. He now lives in Johannesburg and is a successful businessman. When not working he makes best use of his private pilot's licence! He is married with two daughters.

A Whisper in the Reeds is Justin's first book.

A WHISPER IN THE REEDS

'The Terrible Ones' – South Africa's 32 Battalion at War

Justin Taylor

Helion & Company

Co-published in 2013 by:

Helion & Company Limited
26 Willow Road
Solihull
West Midlands
B91 1UE
England
Tel. 0121 705 3393
Fax 0121 711 4075
Email: info@helion.co.uk
Website: www.helion.co.uk
Twitter: @helionbooks
Visit our blog http://blog.helion.co.uk

and

GG Books UK
Rugby
Warwickshire
Tel. 07921 709307
Website: www.30degreessouth.co.uk

Designed and typeset by Farr out Publications, Wokingham, Berkshire
Cover designed by Euan Carter, Leicester (www.euancarter.com)
Printed by Henry Ling Ltd, Dorchester, Dorset

Text © Justin Taylor 2013
Photographs and maps © Justin Taylor unless otherwise noted
The publishers wish to acknowledge the kind assistance of Piet Nortje in the preparation
of this book.

ISBN 978-1-908916-58-7

British Library Cataloguing-in-Publication Data.
A catalogue record for this book is available from the British Library.

For details of other military history titles published by Helion & Company Limited
contact the above address, or visit our website: http://www.helion.co.uk.

We always welcome receiving book proposals from prospective authors.

I have written this account of my experience in the South West African/Angolan Border War for my two daughters, Belinda and Sarah. May they understand me a little better for it, learn from it and if possible, draw inspiration from it. After all, though they weren't born at the time, my motivation for fighting the war was to make the world a better place – for them.

Contents

List of photographs

Black and white photographs

List of maps

Foreword

In this account of his National Service year with South Africa's unique and exceptional 32 Battalion, Justin Taylor deals with this part of our history honestly and compellingly. Caught up in a unit where his work as a Signals Officer placed him at the heart of combat and adventure, but also suffering and death, his story is his own; it takes him from headquarters to bush-base, from training to actual combat, from convoy to home.

His most fascinating remembrance is as a rookie Signals Lieutenant, awakening to the harsh and disturbing realities of a battalion attack on an entrenched enemy brigade, which betrays the innocence, but also portrays the adaptability and guts of so many South African soldiers of the Border War era. During the legendary, but totally unconventional attack on Savate, in the middle of the southern Angolan bush, Taylor and his fellow soldiers, many of whom were equally young and inexperienced, saw and experienced what few other South Africans had encountered. He writes with uncommon feeling about his duties, the slog, the heady combat, and friends and comrades who fought together, and then the pathos and bewilderment as shock, tragedy, and loss strike home amid all the courage and boldness.

In a small way, this short, truthful journey back into old loyalties and a forgotten war evokes the same kind of poignant emotions and empathy which made the book *Fireforce* by Chris Cocks such an unforgettable experience.

This account is worth reading, because it's of a time worth remembering.

Lieutenant-Colonel Willem Ratte
Former Rhodesian SAS;
Commanding Officer, 32 Battalion Reconnaissance Group
May 2011

Foreword

"A Signals Officer's Bush War!" One might ask … "Who is this 'glamour boy' signaller writing this personal recollection and story"? When I first read this memoir in May 2010, I again realized that Justin Taylor certainly earned the right to tell the story about his service and experience with 32 Battalion, and indeed, he tells it with little glamour.

Before I met Justin, I had heard about him. Some of my 32 Battalion Reconnaissance Wing (Recce Wing) comrades, after they returned from the Derico operation, mentioned that the battalion had a new *Engelsman* ('Englishman') Signals Officer who was to arrive at the Omauni base, sometime soon, to receive 'in post' training from the Recce Wing men. On completion of this training, at the end of February 1980, he was most definitely a different *Engelsman* leaving for the Battalion headquarters in Rundu. Not only did his training cover tactical signals but also other combat subjects, preparing Justin to become more operationally prepared for deployments when he accompanied the Battalion commander, Commandant (nowadays Lieutenant Colonel) Deon Ferreira, codename Falcon, into the field. During his short stay at the Omauni base Justin became "one of us". I will never forget his eagerness to learn and participate in training.

Soon after, he deployed on his second operation – one of many to come. He was the first Signals Officer to go on patrol with the companies, and as a bonus saw much action. How many Signals Officers can say that they were in a firefight with the enemy? As time progressed, Justin became Falcon's right-hand man. Whenever Falcon deployed on an operation, Justin would accompany him. Why? An easy answer. This National Service Signals Officer achieved what previous Signals Officers could not – a well-structured signals office functioning effectively in both the heart of the unit's headquarters and also in the field with the tactical headquarters (Tac HQ) affording to all 24-hour tactical radio communication.

As was the case for many Three-Two Battalion men, the Battle of Savate in May 1980 was probably his biggest test, not only in maintaining radio communication, but also the mental and physical challenges of combat. The relationship he built with Falcon was second to none. During the chase of the

18

fleeing defenders of Savate, Justin stayed beside Falcon. As normal, Falcon would follow his own plan, but only after asking Justin's opinion! Justin's recollection of the battle speaks of courage, commitment and grief after losing close friends. Being wounded himself, Justin was only evacuated two days later. In the meantime he maintained radio communication with the headquarters. The story of the Battle of Savate in this memoir is the most complete I've ever read. In order to write such a complete memoir, after all these years, and to remember the detail of such a complex attack, shows what impact this action had, not only on a young National Service Officer, but also on the other battle-hardened career officers.

The end of Justin's National Service period came much too soon. He ended his time with Three-Two, assisting with the orientation-training phase for the newly-arrived junior leaders. Before this, he took the new Signals Officer and signallers to the Omauni base for an intensive training course; this time around he was an instructor on the course. By now he was a well-respected Signals Officer, having earned himself a Chief of the SADF Commendation medal (Later re-titled the Military Merit Medal and abbreviated to MMM).

Justin wrote this memoir primarily for his daughters. However, he has allowed me to use it as a reference work for my next book on 32 Battalion. This unselfish act helped me to draft a more complete piece of work; I can only wish more former 32 Battalion men to be of his calibre. This account is now a valuable part of the 32 Battalion story and by writing this memoir Justin is preserving valuable history.

I know Falcon missed him once he had "*klaared* out" (completed National Service). I clearly remember one evening in early 1981 when he was struggling to speak to Willem Ratte, who was deployed somewhere in Angola. In the Omauni's recce base command bunker he shouted "get me Justin!" only then to realize he was no longer with the battalion.

Regimental Sergeant-Major Piet Nortje
Former 32 Recce Group member and later RSM 32 Battalion
Author of *32 Battalion: The Inside Story of South Africa's Elite Fighting Unit*
Victory at a Price: 32 Battalion's Battle for Savate
32 Battalion: The Terrible Ones
May 2011

Preface

Sometimes things just have a way of playing themselves out. This story is a journey, a journey through a time that saw our country transformed from the pariah of the world to a shining example of tolerance and forgiveness; a journey that so stunned us who were part of it, that we are only now accepting its significance and allowing ourselves our pride. Within this journey is the story of my acceptance as a young man of the winds of fate in the face of the unthinkable; and the discovery of an army Battalion that seems to have epitomised the transformation of Southern Africa – from an age of conflict and despair to one of hope and integrity.

As much as this is a reflection of my personal experience, at a time of enormous change, it is more the telling of a Battalion which, while it may be no longer, is a unit that is so unique that its spirit will forever be out there in the savannahs and forests of Africa …

However, it is still my story.

Lieutenant Justin S.W. Taylor
June 2012

Acknowledgements

I would like to acknowledge Regimental Sergeant-Major Piet Nortje for insisting that I write and document my account of the Battle of Savate for historic reasons. It was this that encouraged me to write about the rest of my time with 32 Battalion.

I would also like to thank Judy, the kindest, sweetest, gentlest soul, for giving me the encouragement and space to write this story.

Maps

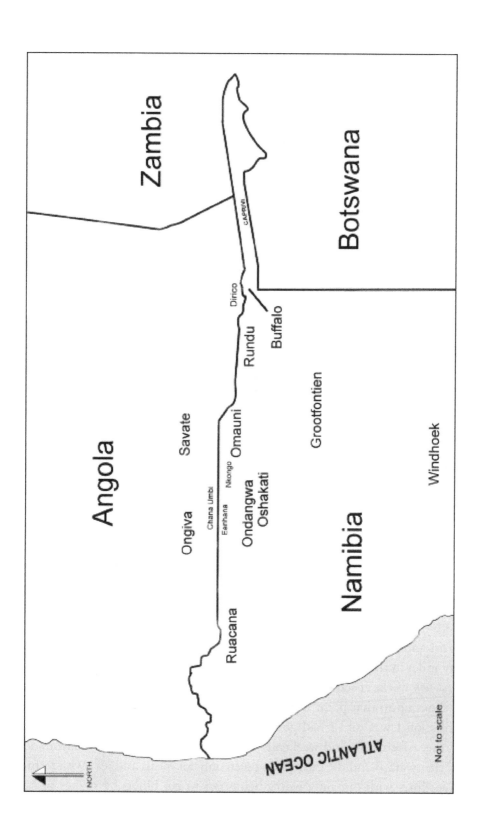

1
Amongst the Zulus

Those early years growing up on a farm in Zululand, South Africa, were happy sun-filled days of adventure and discovery. Bare-headed and barefooted, wearing only a pair of khaki shorts and a shirt, my two brothers and I spent each day exploring the magic of the bush and swamplands that surrounded our sugar farm on the banks of the Umfolozi River. Released after breakfast by our mother, we bolted off with our friends and the farm dogs hunting birds, rodents and monkeys … fishing, riding horses and bicycles, climbing trees, building tree houses and racing home-made go-carts. Every night, the sun would set fiery red on the horizon and flock upon flock of duck and geese would fly over, heading into the setting sun and towards the lakes inland from us. As darkness enveloped our home, the bullfrogs would start up with a distant roar and the nightjars would begin to sing their haunting, echoing, melody.

My heritage is Anglo-Saxon, I am 'white' and English-speaking. Our nursemaids were black Zulu women and our friends were the 'Picannins' (a Zulu term for the young herd-boys who tended the cattle), the sons of the Zulus who were the cane cutters on the farm. It is no surprise that we spoke Zulu before we could speak English. Most evenings we were lulled to sleep by our nursemaids with deliciously terrifying Zulu folklore for our bedside stories, where the hyena was invariably the bad guy and the witch was the evil witch doctor.

And then at six years old … school. The local government school for whites only. My Picannin friends had to walk twelve miles to school every day across the farm and over the Umfolozi River, while my brothers and I were driven twenty miles in the opposite direction to the local village, Kwambonambi. For the first few weeks at school, I hobbled around like a cripple. I had hardly ever worn shoes up to that point in my life, and as my feet were covered in warts (an affliction I was told I had got from frogs on the farm), my shoes nearly killed me. Afternoons and weekends … freedom. Back out on the farm and rivers, the swamps and the bush, being seen only for meals and tea. Wonderful, carefree times with our only worry being not to get bitten by snakes or be

Hunting trips at an early age.

Hunting with the Zulus and their dogs.

Me (right) with my two elder brothers. I am looking none too
enamoured about the prospect of boarding school.

taken by the crocodiles that lurked unsuspectingly on the riverbanks.

After two years of 'day school', I was packed off to a boarding school over
a day's drive away, crammed in the back of the car with two brothers and
all a mass of luggage. Halfway there we had to endure agonising shopping
sessions with my mother in the city of Durban for all our school kit. Excellent
private schools though they were, it was confinement … ten years of it. I would
daydream in class, worrying if my horses, dogs and cats were safe, wondering
how my Picannin friends were doing, and wishing I was fishing in the river
or forcing my way through the reeds alongside the Umfolozi River, a gun in
hand and our farm dogs at my heels. Being let loose for our holidays was a
huge release, with the only looming shadow being the day that we would have
to go back to boarding school – a thought I would cram away into the back of
my mind.

As I grew older, my Picannin friends and I grew steadily apart with the
differences in our lives becoming increasingly apparent. I was born into a life of
privilege, with my parents owning the farm we lived on and being white, I was
fed into the political system of privileged 'Whites' Only' schools, universities,
restaurants and beaches. My Picannin friends on the other hand, were born
to be labourers, their families splintered by the political system as their homes
were in distant 'native homelands' or 'reserves', even though they lived and
worked on the farm. They went to second-rate, black-only schools which few
of them stuck out to the end. Most ended up getting work on the farms at an

early age as either cane cutters or tractor drivers. By the time I was a teenager, we had very little in common and our conversations were both uncomfortable and stilted. And my Zulu didn't progress much further than that of a seven-year-old boy who lived for fishing, hunting and horse riding on a Zululand farm.

In my senior school years I became increasingly aware of the racial divide, of the difference between being black or white, and of the politics that characterised living in South Africa in the mid-1970s. Even though the majority of the population was black, they had no political rights and no vote in mainstream South Africa. The minority white population controlled the country politically and economically, whilst the blacks lived in 'homelands', commuting to work in the white areas. They would travel home to their families in the homelands, on long weekends and for their annual holidays. The Afrikaans term for the political system was 'Apartheid' or 'separate living'. This apparently gave blacks a certain degree of control in their 'homelands', with the whites overseeing these homelands and controlling the rest of the country. Apartheid was a system supposedly designed to avoid what had happened in the rest of Africa. With each country's independence from their colonial masters, the Africans had (with a few exceptions) embraced communism and nationalised their countries

Wading up the Umfolozi River.

assets, with the almost immediate result of complete economic chaos and the emergence of a self-declared dictator; invariably appointed, 'President-for-life'. So true democracy with one-man-one vote in South Africa would mean the black man would take power, and we were convinced that our country would therefore follow the rest of Africa.

As the best farmlands were reserved for whites, the blacks were largely excluded from participation in the mainstream economy. This naturally ensured an affront to their dignity amongst other things, and they began to take increasing exception to the system of Apartheid, as did the rest of the world.

It was a powder keg ready to explode. Even the flocks of duck and geese that flew over our house in the evenings had largely disappeared, and the bullfrogs had fallen silent … as if in anticipation of a terrible storm that was gathering on the horizon. It was only the nightjars that still sang their beautiful melody, now seeming to cry out, 'Good Lord … deliver us'.

2
The Apocalypse looms

My formative teenage years were characterised by a civil war that threatened to erupt beneath our feet with the blacks demanding political freedom, and the ever-present danger of our neighbouring countries swarming over our borders to support them. Our neighbours (Angola, Zambia, Botswana, Zimbabwe, Malawi and Mozambique) had by then achieved independence from their colonial masters, and all having embraced communism (except for Botswana) posed an ever-increasing threat to South Africa, with the backing of the USSR and China. To add to this, we were pretty much a pariah country with the West as they considered the political system of Apartheid unpalatable, with the only thing in our favour being that we were vehemently anti-communist. Aligning ourselves to the West meant that South Africa had a positive role to play in the Cold War. As a regional powerhouse, Apartheid South Africa maintained a balance for the West against the communist threat posed by the Russian and Chinese support of our neighbours. It was this trump card that kept us from complete political isolation.

The future we faced as young South Africans was one of uncertainty and one that promised racial conflict, violence and bloodshed. The simmering civil war in South Africa and the escalating Border Wars were like sinister, dark clouds building menacingly on the horizon. As youngsters at the time, we could see no way out. The way we saw it, whichever way South Africa turned, it spelt doom; maintaining Apartheid meant war; true democracy with one-man-one vote meant communism, nationalisation, economic chaos and persecution by the blacks … it was a looming apocalypse from which we could see no hope of escape.

So it was that by the end of the 1970s, white youngsters where beginning to be called up for compulsory National Military Service in ever increasing numbers. And there I was, surprise, surprise … drafted into the army for two years. In 1979, I arrived as an eighteen-year old conscript at the Army's Corps of Signals. I had set my sights on becoming a platoon commander in the infantry and was not particularly enamoured with my posting as a Signaller.

Surprise, surprise… we all began receiving our call up
papers for compulsory Military Service.

Nevertheless, I decided to make the most of it and by the end of my first year,
I graduated from the Army Gymnasium in Heidelberg as a Signals Officer.
However, this wasn't without its challenges.

As an English-speaking, white South African, the product of exclusive
schools which were the equivalent of English public schools such as Rugby
and Eton, I could hardly understand a word of Afrikaans. The South African
Defence Force (SADF) was a military environment dominated by Afrikaans-
speaking whites who understandably took exception to this as both English
and Afrikaans were our official languages. And they certainly hadn't forgotten
their defeat by the British in the Boer War of 1899-1902, and in particular the
unfortunate privations and deaths of their Boer woman and children in the
concentration camps. The brainchild of Lord Kitchener, the camps were his
attempt at bringing the Boer Commandos to heel by depriving them of their
source of succour and resupply. Good thinking from a military perspective
but unforgivable given the deaths that ensued from maladministration and
overcrowding. So even with the unshakeable pride I have of my English heritage,
I – along with the Afrikaners – also have an axe to grind with Kitchener, and

Basic training - bayonet and camouflage training.

Basic training - learning to shoot the R1 rifle.

certainly no less for the blot he has left on the copybook of British fair play.

And so it was that while we were treated fairly, the Basic Army Training we were put through was made even more difficult for the handful of us *Engelsmanne* (Englishman) in our platoon. Added to this, our grasp of Afrikaans was so poor that we couldn't understand the commands being shouted at us … all of which our Afrikaans speaking instructor conveniently mistook for insolence. So we were forever running twice the distance, doing twice the push-ups and carrying twice the weight on our backs. The silver lining of this was that we were soon amongst the fittest in the platoon.

There was many a time in the following year when involved in the real thing, that I looked back at the Basic Training our instructor put us through with gratitude. Not that we saw it that way at the time. He took us on as a bunch of unfit, ragtag civvies from all walks of life and welded us into a platoon of motivated and well-trained soldiers. It was a process that has been developed over millennia, through which countless army recruits had been through before. Our instructor, Corporal Manns, applied himself with alacrity to the age-old task. He was a tall, lean Afrikaans guy whose legs were so long his 'army browns' combat trousers didn't reach the top of his boots. He hammered us day and night for three long months, and as much as we muttered dark words under our breaths, we had a grudging respect for him as he was very

Take the pain … being made to roll over rocks in the grass with full combat gear.

tough, but also very fair. More often than not, when other platoons were back in barracks at the end of the day, he would put us through the muddy obstacle course one more time, or send us over the hill … again. He taught us that we either all came back together at the same time, or not at all. He would trash our bungalow again and again when we were desperately trying to get ready for inspection before sunrise. We learned to work as a team, to be innovative and perhaps most importantly, to be resilient. To never give up … no matter what he threw at us.

After this initial three months of Basic Training, those of us selected for the junior leadership course were despatched to Bivak (pronounced Beefuk), a tented camp five kilometres outside the main base. The harsh, dry, bitterly cold winter on the Highveld had the water in our army tent fire-buckets freeze over and the wind incessantly blew fine sand into our food. And every day we ran the five kilometres into the main army base for our lectures and then five kilometres back in the afternoon. However, that didn't count as 'exercise' as we still did the rest of the stuff; pole PT, the 2.4 km run with full webbing, rifle and helmet, fieldcraft exercises across the veld and the like. So we became even more fit … and we also learned to 'jippo' …

Some of us soon realised that they seldom did a head count when it came to some of the trips into the main army base. So when the shout came to form up in squads that had everyone boiling out of the tents, we would slip round the back and slide into the long brown veld grass. Befitting their design, our 'nutria brown' combat fatigues blended in perfectly and we would disappear into the long grass as we leopard-crawled a couple of hundred metres up the hill. Here we would loiter in the shade of some rocks, watching the squads running at the double along the road to the main base. On their return in the late afternoon, we would appear like magic amongst everyone making for the tents. That was a long five months, where we received a combination of infantry, military communications (Signals) and leadership skills training.

It was surreal making it from the junior leadership course onto the officers' course and being billeted in the officers' mess. Here we had the whole nine yards, with luxury that only stopped short of our own personal batman. We each had our own room with a desk and a cupboard, had our clothes washed and ironed for us, and ate our meals in the fancy officers' mess. We found this sudden change very awkward at first, but it wasn't long before we fitted right in … 'to the manor born' as it were! And the best of it was that we could now take a leisurely walk to our lectures without having to run everywhere at the

Bivak (pronounced 'Beefuk') tented camp with vehicle park and parade ground on the left.

Signals training in the field.

double or be harassed by screaming NCOs. We noticed with amusement that there was a subtle shift in the attitude of the NCO instructors, as they realised that if we got through the officers' training course and successfully received our commissions, they might just end up reporting to us. Ninety of us made it through the intensive two-month course, graduating as signals officers with the gazetted rank of Second Lieutenant.

Hardly had my pampered life as an officer begun than it came to an end. I volunteered for duty in the combat zone on the 'border', that of Angola and Namibia (then South West Africa). Against the wishes of the United Nations and its Resolution 235, granting independence to South West Africa, South Africa had taken upon itself to extend indefinitely the role of administering the country. This administrative 'responsibility' had been implemented after World War II and, as a result, South Africa had become drawn into fighting a guerrilla war. These guerrillas or 'terrorists', were the Angolan-based SWAPO (South West African People's Organisation), insurgents that were trying to free South West Africa from the 'colonial' rule of South Africa. Just over a dozen Signals Officers were required for duty on the border, with the rest getting comfortable postings to army bases in South Africa. Those of us who stepped forward for border duty fell far short of the numbers required, and so they had to 'volunteer' additional Signals Officers to achieve the manning levels required. The irony for me was that whilst most of my fellow officers were jostling to get posted to bases in South Africa ... I dreaded the prospect. The thought of spending the next fourteen months stuck in a regular army unit, with all its spit and polish and the 'Yes SAH ... no SAH!' discipline that went with it filled me with dismay. Even though in quiet moments I found the prospect of being sent to the Operational Area daunting, I longed for the adventure, the challenge, the open spaces and wild African bushveld. I suppose I had also quietly made up my mind that I would rather fight the external threat with its communist backing, than risk having to police the evolving civil war that was gaining momentum through unrest and riots in the black South African townships.

After two weeks of glorious home leave, having completed the Officers' course, at the end of 1979 we reported to the air force base at Waterkloof in Pretoria. Here we were to catch the three-hour flight up to the border in the Air Force's big camouflaged Hercules C130 (known affectionately as 'flossies') and Transall C160 aircraft. Sitting on our kit in the hot sun alongside the runway, we had time to reflect on the fourteen months that lay ahead. Being

Signalmen Taylor and Saul at the RV waiting for the pickup.

Officers' course – wargames.

Officers' course - CO Wareham shaving … to be an "An Officer and a Gentleman"

Signals Officers it was unlikely that we would be exposed directly to combat, but we were well aware of the fact that this was a very real war, and we carried quite a responsibility as junior officers to ensure that there was adequate communications for the front line units to which we were to be assigned.

At that stage we had no idea where we would be posted once we got to the border. I had heard some intriguing things about a guy I was at school with, who had been part of an army battalion based in the Caprivi Strip, which very few people knew much about. The story was that he had been sent on a reconnaissance mission into Angola which had gone horribly wrong and that the promised hot extraction helicopters had not materialised. Vastly outnumbered, the ensuing escape and evasion experience had so traumatised him that he lost his nerve and was repatriated back to a regular army unit in South Africa. He had lasted about three months with the battalion. The unit he had been part of was the mysterious 32 Battalion, led by white South African officers and NCOs, it was made up of black Portuguese-speaking Angolans who had been extricated from the Angolan Civil war in 1975. Their activities appeared to be obscure missions into Angola, whose border neighboured South West Africa and with whom we were officially not at war.

While the unknown element of the Battalion both intrigued and intimidated me, my intuition told me that the unconventional nature of the unit was where my destiny lay. In addition, my father and grandfather had both been fighter pilots in the two respective World Wars, so I wanted to 'do my bit' as it were and experience a similar challenge.

There was also something about the mystique around the Battalion that drew me irresistibly to it and I set my sights firmly on getting posted to 'Three-Two'.

3

'Three-Two'

On arriving in the big transport plane or 'Flossie' at the huge rear echelon logistics base at Grootfontein in South West Africa, all the Signals Officers and NCOs were called in to a large hall. We were each asked to stand up in turn and indicate our preference for Comcen (Communication Centre) or Tactical Signals. Comcen were the rear-echelon Divisional and Brigade-level Communication Centres, whereas Tactical Signals were the front line Battalion-level communications. With my surname being near the end of the alphabet, I had plenty of time to work out that this would determine where we would be posted. The thought of being stuck in an air-conditioned Comcen hundreds of miles back from the real war filled me with dread – I had to get into the bush. When called upon, I stood up ... "My preference is for Tactical Signals ... and I would like to go to 32 Battalion, Commandant". There was a deathly hush. "What do you know about 32 Battalion Lieutenant?" "All I know is that they work mostly in Angola with black Portuguese-speaking troops, Commandant". There was another pregnant pause as I stood thinking that I had overstepped the mark. In a stage whisper that carried to the back of the hall, he turned to his snickering side-kicks "*Manne* (men), we have us here a *REAL* Captain Caprivi!" My heart sank as I thought I had really cooked my goose. When the names were read out with their postings, he singled me out and made me stand up again. "Taylor ... *ja kerel* (yes boy), Rundu, and 32 Battalion" he said ominously. "Shit!" I thought, "Does he know something I don't?"

I had to wait a few days to get the next flight up to Rundu. When I arrived it was into a scene reminiscent to that in the film *Platoon* when Charlie Sheen arrived in Vietnam. Looking out I could feel the blistering heat and see the dry African bush stretching endlessly from the other side of the simmering tar runway. As we disembarked down the ramp of the Transall C160, the troops '*Klaaring* out' were boarding the plane. Never having seen any of them before, I looked carefully at the 32 Battalion guys going home. They stood quietly to one side, wearing their now faded camouflaged berets with the Buffalo insignia. While they were still strong healthy young men, their measured, deliberate movements betrayed their fatigue. Yet they had an unassuming confidence about them that belied their age and they carried the unmistakable air of the legendary bush fighters the unit was famed for. Long stretches in the African bush interspersed with intense firefights with the enemy had clearly left their mark. I was determined to make it into the unit, and even more determined to live up to their standards.

The handful of us sent up from Grootfontein, were called into the Signals Officers' office at Sector 20 HQ, Rundu. The Captain there started talking about all sorts of units we were going to, not mentioning 32 Battalion. When I respectfully informed him of the fact that I was posted to Three-Two he went apeshit … "No one tells me how to run my outfit and you can be sure you aren't going to that fucking Battalion, who do you fucking think you are and what is so special about fucking 32 Battalion!!" he ranted and raved. "*Jusslyk!*" I thought, "what is it about this unit that gets up everyone's nose?" I spent an uncertain few days, seriously pissed off about having got this far only to be thwarted by what appeared to be the Captain's dented ego. He eventually got over himself and dispatched me to Three-Two …

I walked tentatively down to the Battalion HQ alongside the airfield. On introducing myself as the new Signals Officer I was met with "Oh OK, there's your office" and then was largely ignored for the first week. The Officer Commanding (OC), Commandant Deon Ferreira (also known by his code-name 'Falcon'), finally found the time to call me into his office. He watched me with a bemused look while he introduced me to the unit and wished me luck. I had briefly met the previous Signals Officer on his way out. He had largely left the signals to sort itself out while he played at commander of any logistics convoy that happened to be running between the various border bases. There was a lot to be done to get things in order. I was therefore thankful for the quiet time over Christmas of 1979, using it to find my feet with regards to the administration of the run-down signals unit. I established a firm friendship with another *Engelsman* in the HQ, 2Lt Tim Patrick, who had gone to the same school as me back in SA. He was with our intelligence guys.

It wasn't long before I realised that I fitted right in to the way things were done at Three-Two. I had really battled with the 'spit-and-polish' Army discipline of basic training. Here, the discipline was focused on what really mattered and where it counted – combat-readiness for the bush war being fought. There was respect for rank, but beyond that, everyone got on with the job at hand in a relaxed, efficient manner. The Battalion HQ at Rundu was housed in a large hanger-like corrugated iron building that had been divided into offices without ceilings; the exception being the OC's which had both a ceiling and air-conditioning. The only other air-conditioned room was the sandbagged 'Ops Room' or command bunker on the one end. Wall-to-wall and floor-to-ceiling maps covered most of it, with the maps depicting troop deployments and the Battalion's kills or 'head count'; quietly sheltered behind a curtain. No ceilings meant that you got to hear pretty much everything that was going on. The daily bustle was constant and was mainly centred on logistics matters concerning the troops down at the Buffalo training base, across in the Caprivi Strip. This covered a wide range of issues such as their pay, marriages and divorces, wives and children, schooling, recruiting, training, housing, transport and troops that were AWOL (absent without leave). There were some four thousand people at Buffalo (troops and their families) and everything came back through the HQ at Rundu, to then go on up to Sector level (Sector 20, Rundu) or further back to the giant logistics base in Grootfontein ... or, if necessary and circumstances required such, all the way back to South Africa.

There was a patch of very green grass leading to the apron of the airfield. The feeling of constant activity was heightened by the fact that all the aircraft would park out front if they weren't squirreled away in a hanger; the giant transport Hercules C130s and Transall C160s, the Alouette troop and gunship helicopters, the Pumas and the infrequent Super-Frelon helicopters, the Bosbok spotter and Kudu light transport planes. And of course the jet fighters, occasionally Mirages, but more often the Impala ground strike aircraft. Only foot traffic specific to us came through our gate, with most of it being channelled around us into the greater Rundu base.

I was billeted in the regular army officers' mess. Little did I realise how little time I would actually get to spend there during the course of the next thirteen months. It was also interesting getting used to wearing the distinctive 32 Battalion camouflage beret. As it had just been casually handed to me in the first week, I was initially a little uncomfortable wearing it as I felt I hadn't 'earned my stripes' as it were. Surprisingly quickly, I drew apart from the rest of the junior officers posted with the regular battalions, as I had to be increasingly careful of what I said and how I said it ... and they in turn began regarding me with an increasing mystique.

But there again, Three-Two was a very different army unit. Logistically, it fitted into the regular army structure, but officially (certainly to the outside world at the time) it didn't exist. The Battalion had its origins in the Angolan

Civil War of 1975. The troops were all black Portuguese-speaking soldiers, the remnants of Holden Roberto's FNLA guerrilla army that had fought against the Portuguese colonials. With Angola's independence in 1975, several guerrilla factions began fighting amongst themselves for control of the country, namely UNITA, MPLA, FLEC and FNLA. When Holden Roberto abandoned his FNLA followers, the MPLA faction gained the upper hand. The legendary and esteemed South African Army officer, Colonel Jan Breytenbach, persuaded the South African government to allow him to bring the remnants of the FNLA army into the then South West Africa (Namibia). They eventually found themselves housed in the Caprivi Strip at Buffalo Base and changed their name from Bravo Group to '32 Battalion'. They were led by a white leader group of regular army officers and NCOs. The idea was to use the Battalion primarily for clandestine operations in Angola, given that the rank and file soldiers were Angolans who had been in the FNLA guerrilla army and therefore sworn enemies of the Marxist-backed MPLA government that had taken over from the Portuguese.

For security reasons, the official language of the Battalion was English as the use of Afrikaans would immediately point to South Africa. As my Afrikaans still wasn't too good this suited me just fine! We were officially not at war with Angola, so our activities there were very sensitive. Our dual role was to hunt down the SWAPO guerrillas in their bases in Angola before they came south into South West Africa (Namibia) on the one hand, and to support Jonas Savimbi and his UNITA guerrillas in their ongoing civil war against the ruling MPLA government in Angola (with their FAPLA military wing), on the other.

Commandant Deon Ferreira had taken command of the Battalion in 1979 and under his leadership, the unit had undergone extensive retraining. Honing their basic infantry skills, and entrenching the basic disciplines required to be effective anti-guerrilla fighters, the unit was set to become acknowledged as the 'finest fighting unit in the SADF since World War Two'. This accolade was bestowed on the Battalion by Lieutenant General Jannie Geldenhuys, Chief of the SADF. On Christmas Day 1984 Geldenhuys handed a specially-made plaque to the unit (see colour section).

Under Falcon's command, 1980 marked the year the Battalion began showing its true offensive mettle.

4

Dirico

Come mid-January, I was thrown right into the deep end. Falcon called me to his office and briefed me on the offensive operation being planned against the Angolan town of Dirico. It was midway between Rundu and the Caprivi to the east, nestled in the confluence of a river that ran down from the north to join the mighty Kavango River that formed the border. We were to attack 400 Angolan army troops (FAPLA), with approximately 350 men, in a clandestine operation – we were supposedly to be UNITA guerrilla troops who were fighting the Angolan government. The plan was to cross the river in assault boats in the early hours of the morning, attacking the trenches in a frontal infantry assault at first light. I left Falcon's office in a daze. The enormity of the responsibility that I had in planning the communications fit for the entire Battalion hit me like a steam train. I was disturbed by the fact that I was to be part of an organisation planning to attack and annihilate over 400 men. In addition, they belonged to a regular army battalion of a neighbouring country with which we were not officially at war. I was so overwhelmed by it all I couldn't even think about drafting my signals orders till the next morning. I sat at my desk staring into the middle distance for a while and then walked quietly alongside the runway as the sun went down, collecting my thoughts, considering what lay ahead.

In the morning, I put aside my emotions and produced my first set of signals orders for an offensive operation. After a few adjustments these were signed off by the OC. All the senior officers had moved down to our training area at Buffalo Base in the Caprivi and I was tasked with collating the complete set of battle orders, including my signals orders. I was due to be flown by a Kudu light aircraft down to Buffalo, mid-afternoon. But I misplaced the folder containing the battle orders as they somehow went missing in the morning and as my panic rose, I could see myself not just being court-martialled, but shot! They eventually turned up in the nick of time, being found in the intelligence room somewhere.

We flew uncharacteristically high (about 6,000 feet) as heading east we were not transiting a 'hot' or hostile area this side of the border. I finally found time to read my first letter from my girlfriend back home. Sitting high in the sky, the African bush stretched away endlessly in hues of purple-grey, as the sun sank golden-orange towards the horizon. Alone in the back of the aircraft and faced with the prospect of going into battle for the first time, it was with much emotion that my mind was drawn to loved ones back home … after all, this was why we were fighting the war up here … wasn't it?

It was with great relief that I handed the battle orders over to a senior officer when we landed at the bush strip at last light. The orders were presented that evening to the officers and NCOs by Commandant Ferreira and he asked me to present the signals orders, with no warning … dropping me firmly into the deep end!

We left in a convoy of Buffels in the morning. I was heading for the command vehicle when I realised that I had never fired a shot with my brand new R1 (FN) rifle. I quickly rushed around to the back of the Tiffies' workshop, where there was a deep pit, and fired a full magazine into the opposite sand wall. The automatic rifle worked flawlessly, I just hoped that it would be accurate out to a hundred metres on its factory settings as I just didn't have time to set the sights. I climbed up into the Buffel and sat wiping the factory grease off the rifle. It was to serve me well in the year to come, never letting me down with a stoppage or misfire. I looked after it with a passion and I was to owe my life to both its reliability and deadly accuracy.

We arrived at the area opposite the garrison town of Dirico shortly after nightfall and began moving quietly into position. With the Battalion deployed on the Namibian side of the Kavango, ready to assault in raiding craft just before dawn, I found to my horror that no-one could use the HF radios due to interference on the frequencies I'd been allocated. I had naïvely and blindly accepted that the frequencies supplied by Sector HQ would work – so I hadn't tested them, a procedure we hadn't been adequately trained to do back in South Africa. At about three o'clock in the morning, I was summoned to the group of officers sitting under the bushes with Commandant Ferreira. He spoke quietly and menacingly from the starlit shadows. "*Seiner*, if you don't get comms in the next thirty minutes, I'm throwing you out of the Battalion".

Fuck! He might as well have just punched me in the face! Being thrown out of the unit was one thing, but for me there were few insults that ranked with being called *Seiner* (the Afrikaans word for Signaller). That was what I was, but it was the tone with which it was used that got me going … insinuating we were good-for-nothing "jam stealers" sitting safely back in base. But there again ... no comms ... he was right ... I was clearly deep in the shit and had no clue how I was to get myself out of it. I rushed around fiddling with antennas and different radios – not much helped. I even prayed, hard, making all sorts of promises to the Big Fella. To this day I still do not know how, but before my allotted time was up, we were able to communicate, albeit with our voices sounding not unlike the Donald Duck cartoon character. A little later, with barely half an hour to go before boarding the assault craft, the attack was called off by the brass in Pretoria. Apparently, it seems most of the garrison were reported not to be in the base, but I am not convinced that this was the real reason.

I was tasked to remain behind with the three CSI (Chief Staff Intelligence) operatives while Lt Willem Ratte and his team went in to blow the bridge leading to the town. I arrived at the little fishing hut where Commandant Oelschig and his operatives were bunked. Oelschig was an energetic, intelligent and resourceful officer with an enthusiastic spring to his step. The hut was nestled amongst the trees on the Kavango River opposite Dirico, overlooking the confluence of the two rivers. They took one look at me, brand new everything ... rifle, camouflage combat fatigues (as worn by Three-Two when on external Ops) and my green Machilla (an H frame back-pack used exclusively by the Battalion). I was out to show that I was tough, I could hack it, and that I could take anything. Being permanent force soldiers, they had seen this all before. They decided to teach me a lesson I have never forgotten ... "Any fool can be uncomfortable in the bush". They had sheets on their camp beds, hot meals and ice with their drinks in the evenings. I was left to sleep outside the hut on the sand, drinking warm water from my water bottles and scratching through very basic rat-packs for my meals. I wasn't even allowed to sit on any of their camp chairs, but left to sit in the sand with my back against a rough tree ... listening to the enticing chink of ice in their glasses! I ignored my discomforts and with grudging respect, accepted their 'initiation'.

With the CSI guys comfortably ensconced in their beds, I spent long hours alone sitting outside in the bush with my rifle across my lap, peering out over the big river. Somewhere just out there, in the vast reed beds that bordered the river on all sides, Willem and his team were packing explosives under the bridge. In the breathless, starlit night, I wondered how they were doing, hoping they would pull it off safely as they were uncomfortably close to the enemy base. I also got to thinking about those back home, why we were fighting the war and pondering what the year ahead held in store for me. As if in reply, the reeds that were standing silvery-still in the moonlight, would mysteriously move in unison as a breeze gently brushed their tips in restless, rolling waves that were seemingly everywhere and yet nowhere. It was both soothing and disturbing ... provided explanations that were questions, hinted at hidden strengths and lurking dangers ... and the reeds seemed to be rustling as if in a whisper. Ever since that night on the banks of that mysterious river, the magic of the wind whispering in the reeds has for me epitomized the very soul of Three-Two.

Willem Ratte and his men had been ferried by Zodiacs (inflatable raiding craft) across the main Kavango River early one evening, and had then walked through the marshy countryside of the eastern bank of the Cuito River to the road. They then walked west along the road to the bridge, where Trooper Joao stepped on an old Anti-Personnel mine. Fortunately for him, only the detonator went off; the main charge failed to explode. On getting to the river, they had assembled the canvas and wood Klepper canoes which they had carried with them. Undertaking an initial close target inspection of the bridge that night, they then rowed quietly down the river to hide in the reeds, well concealed and out of range of the Dirico garrison. After lying up for the day and preparing their explosives, they returned after last light to the bridge, and began attaching the charges to the bridge pillars.

One of the guys with Willem told me later that he was posted as lookout on the bridge on that final night. At just after midnight, he was instructed to shoot the FAPLA sentry with his silenced AK-47 which was equipped with a night sight. This he duly did, but things got progressively tenser as he then despatched the relief sentry, and then the sentry who ambled lazily down to see what had become of the first two. It was with great relief that he was summoned to join the rest of the team in the boats down below. Quietly slipping away in their Klepper canoes they rendezvoused with the Zodiacs further down the river.

Just before dawn, we saw the brilliant and searing white flash of the explosion on the horizon, long before we heard the echoing boom that thundered down over the reed beds and across the wide expanse of river.

5

Retraining

It was a long and bumpy trip back from Dirico to the HQ in Rundu in a Buffel armoured vehicle. I kept a low profile, hoping the OC wasn't still after my blood. I pulled out all the signals manuals, collected three Signallers together and quietly organised a Buffel to take us west to Omauni, our recce wing base. I had never been there before, but instinctively knew that this was where I would get the training I needed. Our own recce wing was comprised of sixty handpicked men from within the Battalion, of whom about twenty were white officers and NCOs. They were led by Lieutenant Willem Ratte – an ex-Rhodesian SAS member and one of the most capable soldiers I ever worked with. Willem was a tall, lanky guy with thick glasses, curly blond hair and a quiet, unassuming, demeanour. An educated man with a Bachelor of Arts degree in teaching, he was an unlikely looking soldier at first take. I had enormous respect for him due to his measured, professional and balanced approach to the job at hand. The courage he displayed time and time again never ceased to amaze me. Under his leadership, Omauni base had a comfortable homely feel to it, underscored by a quiet professionalism that reflected the bases' evident combat readiness.

Just two hundred metres by two hundred metres, Omauni was situated alongside a big, hard-surfaced runway with sand embankments three metres high surrounding it. Raised bunkers at each corner and bunkers set into the embankments in between, bristled with .30 calibre (re-bored to 7.62mm) Browning machine-guns and .50 Browning machine-guns, all of which were in immaculate condition, with fresh crates of ammunition positioned readily to hand. In the centre of the base were two 81mm mortar pits. Both of which were fixed on pre-determined fire patterns in the event of an attack. They would automatically hit all the likely areas the enemy were to approach from, until a more accurate combat appraisal could be made.

The base also featured a sunken sand-bagged command bunker, bungalows for the officers, NCOs and troops, ablutions that featured hot showers and flushing toilets (a luxury, as in most forward combat bases as these were usually the dreaded 'long drop') and a large corrugated-iron mess hall with

Omauni Recce Base and one of the .50 Browning machine guns in an anti-aircraft role ….
"We were armed to the teeth and willed the enemy to attack". (Courtesy of Piet Nortje)

bare concrete floors, benches and the ubiquitous tin army tables with folding legs. Added to this was a workshop, sandbag-covered ammo bunkers and an armoury. And of course there was the pub … a bunker converted into this most important feature with a parachute suspended from the roof as the ceiling and a human skull perched on the bar counter.

With trees scattered around for shade, Omauni also boasted a thatch gazebo in the middle, which was used for tea and coffee. That was my favourite… tea in the gazebo. Every day before sunrise, everyone in the base would move into the bunkers for 'stand-to', quietly manning their positions and scanning their defensive arcs of fire as the sun came up … followed by tea, coffee and rusks in the gazebo. We would meet in the gazebo again late in the afternoon before evening 'stand-to', watching the sun gently setting to the west. Sunrise and sunset was the most likely time for an attack and hence having to 'stand-to'. It wasn't long before I realised how well armed and prepared we were, and began willing the enemy to attack. They never did … they had obviously done their homework and knew to stay away.

Omauni had the usual pets that were treated with a soldier's typical 'rough compassion'. The most notable were Milly the cat and a vervet monkey. The cat was put through a military 'selection course' and parachuted off the eighteen metre high water tower, suspended beneath the canopy of a parachute flare. She passed the course, had kittens and spent many an evening curled up next to the big HF radios in the command bunker. The monkey was a real character. He loved drinking beer with the boys in the pub and the more inebriated he got, the more he struggled to keep his balance; his tail moving horizontally to a 90 degree position as it sought to balance its owner upright! The monkey was a great show-off as well. When we met for tea in the gazebo he would do a dashing display of leaping from the roof into the trees, using the branches to whip himself back up into the next tree ... until the day someone surreptitiously cut the branch just enough to snap as he landed on it. Roars of laughter from the guys in the gazebo only added to his embarrassment ... which only made us laugh even more.

Perhaps the most intriguing aspect of Omauni was the family of about twenty-five bushman that lived outside the base. They lived as they had done for thousands of years, wearing only a loincloth. They slept on the sand under the stars, whilst holding their head up with one arm to stop insects crawling into their ears and they hunted in the bush with bows and arrows. They actually made for an excellent early warning system and also served as a source of information on the goings on in the surrounding area. The quid pro quo was that we would provide them with basic medical care and supply them some rations.

I spent the next week reviewing signals theory and refining our standard operating procedures whilst getting some practical tips from the recce guys. We were lucky to be taken under the wing of a young recce officer who was base commander at the time. He was effectively on R & R, having lost his nerve on a prisoner snatch that had gone wrong in Angola a few months earlier. I can't remember if they got back with any of the Angolan army troops they jumped that night just outside their base in Angola ... it seemed one of them screamed blue murder and managed to extricate himself from his attackers, bolting back towards the nearby army base; I think they may have managed to kill him in the process. The guys in the team made it back together, while the young officer got separated. Sometime later he appeared alone from the bush on the other side of the river that marked the Angolan border, dishevelled and with a wild, disconcerted look in his eye. It was heartrending to see him battling with the traumatic stress of whatever had happened. He would suddenly cut off in mid-sentence, get up and walk off a few metres and stare into the middle distance, returning a few minutes later to say "So where were we … ?" I don't think he ever did come right.

One of the other recce guys training us was Sergeant Piet Nortje. A lean, focused young guy with short cropped hair and fine features, he showed excellent organisational skills even then, given that in the coming years, he would be promoted to be the Regimental Sergeant-Major of Three-Two. No mean feat … as in the process he became the youngest RSM in the history of the SADF.

These experienced professionals gave us basic field craft training officially referred to as 'minor tactics' and upped our skill at arms with a variety of platoon weapons, NATO and Russian, such as the ubiquitous AK-47 assault rifle and the RPD, RPK and PKM machine-guns. They helped me with my battle kit, putting together my 'first line' webbing from bits and pieces we scrounged from corners of the supply store. I was very chuffed with this as the frayed and faded canvas made me look like a real veteran; it was simple, practical and was to serve me well in the years to come. It consisted of shoulder straps attached to a web belt onto which I attached my 9mm pistol in a canvas holster; a water bottle, and pouches for one day's rations and a first aid kit. Over this I strapped my tattered old chest webbing for the four R1 rifle magazines, with pouches on each side for hand grenades. This arrangement dispersed the weight of the equipment and held it firmly against your body, whilst allowing freedom of movement in a firefight.

Our recce instructors began to enjoy this orientation thing as much as we did, and we had almost two weeks of impromptu training from them. This individualized instruction saw me really begin to develop a bond with my brand new R1 assault rifle. I hadn't had much time to 'shoot it in' previously. But now that I was in a forward combat base, I had unrestricted access to a mountain of ammunition, so I would fill all four of my magazines and fire off eighty rounds a day. It was an easy stroll out to the firing range, which was a sand embankment, just a couple of hundred metres from the base.

With the reconnaissance guys giving me pointers, I soon became one with the 7.62mm R1. I learned to place my feet slightly apart, roll onto the balls of my feet and lean slightly into the rifle butt, placing the bead through the peep site fractionally beneath my target. Imperceptivity squeezing the trigger, the recoil would slam back into my shoulder and lift the barrel slightly, only to have it settle naturally back onto the target… and I would squeeze off another round. The weight and balance of the rifle matched its recoil perfectly.

Snap shooting was the order of the day, learning to lead with the first round and kill with the second. I fired mostly at beer cans; placing the bullet in the sand just beneath the tin can and making it jump a metre into the air. As it landed I'd fire the next round beneath it, making it hop into the air again. I followed the tin can as it hopped around on the wall, firing again and again until I had chased it over the bank. Then I would start on the next beer can, until I either ran out of beer cans or ran out of ammunition. The singular action of swinging it up into my shoulder, placing my feet slightly apart, rolling onto the balls of my feet and leaning slightly forward to squeeze off a round became increasingly instinctive. My R1 seemed to become an extension of my arms, and hitting what I was aiming at a reflex action. Carrying the rifle with my fingers curled around the magazine with the barrel pointing to the ground was the most natural, comfortable thing in the world.

I began to cherish these sessions and I stuck to this routine whenever I was in a forward combat base. This discipline was later to save my life. And being cocooned in my earmuffs out on the range firing my rifle was 'my' time, my private space to balance life in the base with troops continually around me. I usually went out in the late afternoon, and when done I would amble back to the base to climb up over the embankment, relaxed and introspective. My evenings were usually a hot shower and an early meal in the mess. Climbing into a comfortable enough bed under a mosquito net in a bungalow shared with three others ensured a good night's sleep, and an early rise at four thirty for stand-to at dawn.

The final stage of our impromptu 'selection course' consisted of being loaded into a Buffel, and the four of us being dropped off on the Angolan border one afternoon. Whilst it wasn't a particularly 'hot' area, we were certainly well in the Operational Area with a reasonable chance of running into some gooks.

We were instructed to walk the 25km back to base, which meant we would spend the night in the bush. The Buffel disappeared back towards Oumani and as the silence of the dry brown bush enveloped us, the full responsibility of my predicament settled firmly on me. I was the leader of a four man 'recce stick', and as a Signals Officer, short on a lot of the basic infantry and reconnaissance skills I would like to have had. The three signallers with me were even worse off, having had very little field training or experience other than the informal training we had recently received! But there again, that's why we were there. So it was that after getting a slap on the back and a few pointers as to how to handle the 'recce' thing from the instructors, I set off with a show of confidence and bravado I certainly didn't feel.

We stopped just before dark to make our scheduled radio report and surprisingly couldn't make comms. I kept calling quietly on the radio, "Zero Alpha this is Bravo One ... Zero Alpha, Zero Alpha this is Bravo One, do you read, over ...". Nothing. We sat there perplexed, a little unnerved at not being able to talk to base, each sitting about ten metres apart, looking quietly and intently out into the menacing bush. The sun set and the darkness immersed us. With our radio unserviceable, we had no contact with the outside world and no hope of support in the event of contact with the enemy. With only four of us, we would almost certainly be outnumbered and being very inexperienced, we felt very alone ... it was going to be a long, long, night. We then moved forward in the dark about five hundred metres and cut back on a dogleg to lie up on our spoor. We lay under a bush in a star formation with our feet together so that we could quickly kick each other awake should the need arise.

Suffice to say, we didn't sleep much that night. We stood to at dawn, quietly watching the surrounding vegetation as the sun rose. Emerging from beneath the bush under which we had taken cover, we moved off shortly after sunrise. An hour later we stopped to make another scheduled radio check with Omauni. Again ... nothing. We checked everything again and again and still couldn't get comms. By mid morning we had intercepted a road and found the fork at which we were to turn left towards the base. With two of us walking either side of the two-track sand road, it wasn't long before we saw very obvious signs of scratching and disturbance in the sand of one of the tracks. We had been told to look out for landmines and informed that should we find one, we would be inevitably ambushed by at least thirty SWAPO guerrillas lying in wait. Everyone spread out and found cover, as I crawled carefully forward to scratch softly in the sand. My finger hit something hard and I scraped the sand away. My blood froze as the olive green corner of a Russian landmine was revealed. I recoiled and slithered backwards, turning outwards to face the imminent enemy attack. A very anxious ten minutes went by ... "What the fuck were they waiting for?" I wondered. I then tried to get comms. I crawled over to my Machilla to try and get the big HF radio working yet again. Not daring to lift my head, I lay on my back and threw the wire antenna by its weight into the tree above me. Not surprisingly, nothing again. I tried the short-range VHF radio, thinking we might be in range of the base. Whether they could hear me or not, I blindly relayed our predicament over the air hoping someone would hear me.

We lay on the sand in the fierce heat of the baking sun with very little cover and the tension mounting … four of us against a possible thirty … with a broken radio and unable to call for back up. We waited for the inevitable; it was simply a matter of time before they opened fire and we were overrun. After about half an hour of the guerrillas not springing their ambush, I began to think of making a run for it. It was just then that we heard a vehicle approaching from the direction of the base and to our relief, saw that it was a Buffel grinding its way through the bush along the road. I ran in a crouch as it got closer to warn them of the landmine and impending ambush – then I saw the huge grins! They had taken us rookies hook, line and sinker. Unbeknown to us, they had swopped our HF radio with an unserviceable one and buried the landmine so carelessly that even we amateurs would spot it. I was too relieved to be pissed off. They had taught us an invaluable lesson and one I was never to forget – and that is what it felt like to be a soldier out in the bush without any form of communications, when your life most depended on it. It motivated me to drive myself more and more in the months ahead to ensure that it didn't happen to any of our guys.

Back in Omauni we spent the next few days wrapping up all that we had learned and the techniques we had worked out. I began refining a process that would minimise the chances of a comms failure such as at Dirico from ever happening again. This entailed my personally testing all the allocated frequencies over a 24 hour period, trying them every 15 minutes to select the ones that worked best at particular times of the day. We would end up typically using an 8 MHz frequency mid-day, dropping to 5 MHz early evening and then down to just over 2 MHz in the early hours of the morning. This was all to do with the earth's ionosphere (off which the HF radio waves would bounce back to earth) rising and falling as the earth's temperature increased during the day and fell at night. As the frequency changed, so did the length of the antenna, and so we used a formula to ensure we had a quarter wavelength with each given frequency. The distance you wanted to communicate over also affected the choice of frequency. I began to realise that under these conditions, there was as much an art to radio telephony as there was a science.

6

My reprieve

By now it was the end of February and a message came through that Commandant Ferreira was on his way and I was to prepare to leave Omauni. My fear was that he was coming to personally throw me out of the Battalion, as he had threatened to do at Dirico. I went out to meet the big Puma on the airfield and await my fate. With the helicopter turbines still winding down in the background, Falcon stopped and looked at me steadily "I hear you have retrained yourself … ??" He then went on to inform me that I was to accompany him to Sector One-Zero, the western part of the Operational Area. With relief, I realised that at last I had won a reprieve.

We joined the Tac HQ in a base that might have been Umbalantu. The radios had already been set up by a very organized Permanent Force signals NCO from a regular infantry battalion. All I had to do was man the radio net for the companies in Angola, up to the north of us. We were part of a much larger force operating just across the border which included regular South African Army platoons, some of whom were 'campers' – Citizen Force guys called up for a three month 'camp'. One helluva thing those camps, living an ordinary life back in civvy street one minute and then only a few days later finding yourself fighting in Angola!

It was on this operation that I first met the legendary gunship pilots Arthur Walker and Neall Ellis. They worked very well as a team and this, combined with the tenacity with which they applied themselves, made them a deadly combination. Arthur Walker was a blond, stocky guy with a boxer's nose who went on to become the only double recipient of South Africa's highest bravery award (Honoris Crux). Neall Ellis was a more suave-looking guy who, some twenty years later, I saw on TV that he was still plying his trade. Only now he had upgraded from the small Alouette gunship and was flying the awesome Russian Hind helicopter gunship for a West African country. As always, he was still intent on subduing rebel fighters!

It wasn't long before one of our platoons hit a contact and we dispatched the Alouette helicopter gunships in support. It so happened that the Chief of the SADF, General Constand Viljoen, was visiting the Tac HQ at the time.

He stood behind my shoulder for the duration of the contact whilst I handled the radio traffic, trying to remain calm and cool. The tactic was to try and get the gooks visual and then initiate the contact just as the helicopter gunships arrived overhead. The ground troops would then advance while the gunships circled above, their deadly 20mm cannons killing any that tried to break away from the pursuit. Some eight guerrilla bodies were brought back by the Pumas sent in at the end of the contact with the ammunition resupply. They were laid out in a row alongside the helipad like broken dolls, all hideously disfigured by the 20mm cannon. One had half his skull blown off, another had an entry hole the size of a large coin in the centre of his chest whereas his back had been blown open by the exiting explosive head of the cannon shell … it was a gruesome and sobering sight.

A few days later it was our turn to take casualties. The 'campers' attached to the regular infantry battalion that was working with our guys in Southern Angola were mortared during the night. They hadn't dug in, which was supposed to be a standard operating procedure and most of one of the platoons had been wounded and a number killed. They were trooped back by the Pumas and laid out on the helipad. Lying on their ground sheets in three rows, some with their shirts removed and their pale white skin looking very fragile and out of place while the medics worked quietly and intently on them. The platoon commander, a Lieutenant, was brought into the Tac HQ unharmed but in a state of shock. I didn't envy him having to live with not having instructed his men to dig in.

On a lighter note, and in complete contrast to the awful events just described, there was a young pet donkey in the base to whom the troops supplied copious amounts of beer. One evening, I arrived back at my tent to find that it had passed out on a bed next to mine! This typified the incredulous world we seemed to be living and fighting in.

7

First combat

About a week later, the OC sent Sergeant-Major Ueckerman (the Battalion's new Regimental Sergeant Major) and I to join one of our platoons in Southern Angola to get 'front line' experience. It was with some trepidation that I waited alongside the Puma helicopter for the pilots to arrive. With the attack earlier in the year planned for Dirico, I had *almost* got over the border into Angola. There had been so much on my mind at the time with the hassles I was having with the communications, that I hadn't had time to think of some the realities whilst sitting in the dark, waiting to board the assault boats. This time, leaning against the chopper … I had all the time in the world to mull it over as I was about to be deployed into the field as a plain infantryman.

I was about to be trooped into a neighbouring country with whom we were officially not at war. We looked nothing like the regular South African army troops who wore nutria brown bush fatigues and carried unpractical, faded green canvas backpacks. We wore our 'external ops' camouflaged battle fatigues with homemade 'first-line kit' – chest webbing for spare magazines, together with a pistol, hand-grenades, emergency medical kit and one day's water and rations attached to a web belt and supported by shoulder straps to carry the weight. The idea was that when you hit a contact, you threw off your rucksack and fought through the action with just your first-line-webbing. This would give you all you needed for a firefight together with a day's supply of food, water and ammunition if you had to make a run for it. The rest of our kit we carried in Three-Two's distinctive green, H-frame 'Machilla' rucksacks. These were packed with a sleeping bag, bivvy (single sheet of nylon that sheltered you from the rain as a 'tent'), ground sheet, five days rat-packs (rations), five water bottles, a 'poncho' raincoat, spare socks (I soon learned to leave the underpants and go 'commando' due to the heat!), spare ammo and, as signallers, spare radio batteries.

We blacked out our faces and hands with 'black-is-beautiful' cream so that our white faces would not stick out as targets amongst our black troops, and wore Portuguese style army caps with an impractical sun flap at the back. We carried no identification so that we could not be linked to South Africa if we were captured or our bodies recovered by the enemy. I chose not to carry an AK-47 as we were encouraged to do for external ops, preferring instead to stick with my R1 rifle. The serial numbers had been ground off our R1s so they could not be traced and the 7.62 mm ammunition we were issued with was specially manufactured in Pretoria, with no identification or batch markings on the cartridges. The boots we wore had canvas sides and no markings on their soles. I was still very self-conscious kitted out with our 'external ops' kit … particularly when I could see the regular army troops stealing surreptitious glances at us, delighting in the fact that they were seeing something they weren't supposed to see. But there again, it felt really cool … hey, this was special mission stuff!

The pilots finally ambled out in their loose fitting, green flying overalls. The turbines spooled up and we lifted off, flying at break-neck speed a few feet above the trees. We soon flashed out over the cut-line that marked the border which was absolutely dead straight for hundreds of kilometres, east to west … and then I was in Angola … politics and moralities aside it was exciting, heady stuff. It was an exhilarating ride as I sat in the door with my feet out on the step as I had seen the Parabats doing, my head being pummelled by the slipstream as I looked out at the treetops rushing by barely a metre below my feet. Really, really suave … until the chopper pilot banked at what felt like ninety degrees to turn in towards the white smoke grenade that had been detonated to mark the position of the platoon. I suddenly found myself looking straight down at the ground and *kakked* ('shat') myself! I grabbed my rifle and the side of the chopper thinking I was going to drop out the door, helped along by the pile of head-high rations and ammo behind me – but the strong centrifugal force kept us all glued to the floor. The pilot expertly straightened out and flared the Puma to land gently on the sand. Trying to look cool with my heart still thumping, I jumped out and at long last my feet were finally planted firmly in enemy territory. With the roar of the blades idling above us we offloaded the resupply of rations and ammunition. The silence was deafening after the helicopter had lifted off, rising up out of a mini sand storm before heading south. It took my ears about twenty minutes to return to normal. From then on I wore ear-muffs whenever I rode in a Puma.

We joined the platoon in the tree line, and looking around I slowly started to pick out some of the men spread out in the bush. After being briefed by the platoon commander about our position in the platoon and our responsibilities,

Three-Two troops boarding a Puma helicopter to be airlifted
into Angola. (Courtesy of Piet Nortje)

we moved off through the bush. Machilla squarely on my back, rifle held at
half port across my chest webbing we walked purposefully on our magnetic
compass bearing. We settled into the daily routine of 'stand-to' at dawn, moving
off just after sunrise with a break every hour. From eleven in the morning we
would siesta until three in the afternoon to sit out the intense midday heat. We
would then move off again, setting up our TB (temporary base) just before
sunset. The platoon of some thirty men would arrange themselves in a circle
with the platoon commander and 60mm mortar guy and radio man in the
middle. Each soldier would dig a slit trench in the soft sand about half a metre
deep and two metres long to sleep in, feet to the middle and head facing out.
We would all 'stand-to' as the sun set – this entailed every man being on guard
and ready to fend off any potential attack at sun-up and sunrise, as this was the
most likely time for an assault on our position.

After the deep black night had enveloped us we would have our dinner.
This was my best time … absolute silence in the vast expanse of bush. Safely
enveloped by the darkness, I would prepare a hot meal from my Rat-packs. My
only utensil was what we called an 'Ops knife' which was a Swiss Army knife
we were issued with. I would use the blade as a knife, tea-spoon and fork; the
latter by turning the blunt side of the knife against the side of my mouth. I
opened tin-cans, cut my nails and tightened screws on my rifle with it. Our

Rat-packs had bully beef, baked beans, tinned vegetables, army biscuits, sweets, soup, tea and coffee. I would conserve my water during the day by taking small sips so as to have a full 'fire-bucket' of tea after sunset – my logic being that my body would conserve more moisture this way than if I drank it during the heat of the day. I would sit with my feet in my slit-trench, elbows on my knees and with the night offering me a moment of privacy away from the platoon, I would savour every mouthful of the sweet, milky liquid. Looking out into the surrounding bush I would marvel at how much I could see in the darkness … and at how peaceful it was. We always spoke in whispers as the drone of normal conversation carried an uncanny distance. It was weird getting back to base and getting used to talking normally again, as you would instinctively lapse into a whisper!

Ablutions were an issue. Taking a leak was easy … just remember to piss against a tree, close up and at an angle so as it doesn't make a noise. Anything more serious was a problem. We were encouraged to do our business inside the platoon perimeter for obvious safety reasons. However, I needed my privacy and so this was something I struggled to do. I would therefore go to great lengths to organise an outer perimeter excursion. Yet, I was always very conscious of the incident whereby one of our sergeants did just that and whilst squatting outside the perimeter, some gooks opened fire on his platoon. As the rounds began to fly, he was mistakenly shot through the foot by one of his own troops and landed right in the shit … literally. With this in mind, one postponed these expeditions until they were absolutely necessary.

Near the end of the first week, I had my first contact. We spotted some gooks on the other side of a *chana*, just inside the tree line. A *chana* was a slight indentation in the flat expanse of bush and was usually a couple of hundred metres across. In the rainy season it had ankle deep water in it, but at this time of year it had just dried up. While we were working our way around the side of the *chana*, one of our platoon sergeants opened fire prematurely. The gunships had not arrived overhead so we immediately lost the tactical advantage and were not able to corner the insurgents between the ground troops and the gunships. In an effort not to completely lose the initiative, with Sergeant Major Ueckerman next to me, the platoon commander ordered us to charge over the open *chana* in a wild, zigzagging run. We started a semblance of fire and movement as we hit the tree line, moving through the enemy TB (temporary base). All we got for our trouble was one wounded gook, the rest having made good their escape, bomb-shelling into the bush away from us. It was sobering to see the tatty condition of the gook's equipment and it made me appreciate the hardships our enemy had to endure. In one of their abandoned backpacks were some new brassieres, no doubt the gook was taking these back for his lady?!

Our SWAPO adversaries were the quintessential guerrilla fighters, tough as nails, living off the land and attacking only when it suited them. Once out in the bush, they did not have the luxury of resupply every five days, let alone helicopter gunship support in the event of a contact or medical evacuation if they were wounded. After a contact with us they ran, and kept running, either outstripping us, or dying. This war was tough enough, even the way we were fighting it, yet these guys took it to the next level. It was hard to hate them. In fact, I found myself feeling a certain amount of compassion and a huge dose of respect for them.

One of the AK-47 assault rifles we picked up was in pretty good nick and I kept it as my personal 'Eastern Bloc' weapon … however, I very seldom took it on Ops with me as I far preferred my R1. Falcon was pleased that Sergeant Major Ueckerman and I had been 'blooded', even if he was a little dismissive about the paltry fight the gooks had put up.

I also learned an invaluable lesson about booby traps on that first time in Angola. Whilst on patrol I spotted a Chinese pineapple grenade lying innocuously in the sand. My eyes lit up as this would be a really cool souvenir. As I moved to pick it up, the black Portuguese-speaking troop next to me urgently indicated that I should stop. In sign language and the odd English word he indicated that it might be booby-trapped … and so we made a wide birth around it and moved on. From then on, I avoided anything 'interesting', even if it didn't look suspicious. I am sure what that troop taught me that day avoided me being maimed in the times to follow and in fact, probably saved my life. Booby traps were prolific. Around that same time, one of our platoons found a food cache stored in a bunker in Southern Angola. I was manning the Tac HQ at the time and we instructed them to avoid it, at all costs, until the engineers arrived by helicopter. This took a good few hours to arrange … . the platoon leaders (a Lieutenant and a Sergeant) inevitably got bored and sneaked into the entrance of the cache … one died from the explosion and the other had his legs hideously disfigured. Jam tins filled with pieces of reinforcing rod, cut at an angle, made for a deadly booby trap when detonated by trip wire.

Being on patrol with Three-Two was cool. You settled into a good routine that didn't push you physically too much. We slept well, ate well, and were

"When the shooting starts, it's not the colour of the man's skin
next to you that counts, it's what he is capable of."
Three-Two Battalion… black Portuguese-speaking Angolans with white South
African officers and NCOs. Pictured above are members of Three-Two's Recce
Group (1982). Adding to the diversity of this particular team, of interest is that the
three South Africans are all of different extraction: Jewish, English and Afrikaans.
L to R Standing: Rifleman Mario Hangolo; Rifleman Bambi; Corporal Martin
Jordan, Sergeant Peter Williams, Corporal Patrick Rolf, Rifleman Augustinhos.
L to R Seated: Rifleman Paulino; Rifleman Inácio; Rifleman Dumba
(Courtesy of Sergeant Dave van der Merwe, 32 Battalion Recce Group)

well-armed and organised. If a platoon hit a contact they would immediately
radio for helicopter gunship support which usually arrived within 20 minutes.
With the gunships circling above, the gooks would duck for cover under some
bushes. From here they would be flushed out by the ground troops moving
line abreast through the contact area. If they broke cover and ran before the
troops got there, they were usually taken out by the gunship above. It would
become a turkey shoot if the timing between the gunships and ground troops
was right. The trick was to find them in the vast expanse of featureless bush
and soft white sand and only then initiate the fire-fight when the gunships

arrived overhead, or else the gooks would bombshell in every direction. After a contact, the platoon would then be resupplied with ammunition and rations, with the wounded and, mostly, enemy dead carried back by the resupply Puma helicopters.

Even to my rookie eye, I could see that our troops ranked with the best bush fighters in the world. Not dissimilar to the British Army's Gurkhas, they were professional soldiers doing it for a living – just without typical British pomp and ceremony. Ours was a down-to-earth and practical approach. And I began to notice something very different and very unique about Three-Two. With the political system of racial segregation imposed by Apartheid still alive and well back in South Africa, I slowly realised the subtle difference that set us apart … that there was absolutely no discrimination in the Battalion. Reliance upon each other for survival and the resulting respect for each other's abilities soon marginalised any racial barriers between black and white. And this came directly from the top too … Commandant Ferreira would get extremely agitated if there was any hint of discrimination against his troops. He insisted on absolute and total equality, which was in stark contrast to any other army unit or the official policies in place back home.

Sergeant Major Ueckerman and I were trooped back out of Angola after ten days on a regular 'rat-run'. Arriving back on the big Puma, it was good to see the pet donkey still wandering around, and being late afternoon he was still sober. A good shower and a steaming hot monster meal in the mess was followed by a cracking session in the pub, where we happily smashed a good few beers into our faces!

Three-Two Battalion embodied a steady, methodical, no nonsense, and practical approach to the task at hand. The discipline was focused on the essentials such as bush craft, basic hygiene, cleanliness and the operational readiness of our weaponry as opposed to all the usual regular army spit and polish stuff. Our strategic and tactical approach was based on the principles of only attacking under conditions that were favourable to us and the adoption of a 'live to fight another day' philosophy … and this clearly suited me just fine!

We knew we were something special, something unique and we carried this attitude with very little ego … we were intensely proud to be a part of the unit.

8

Ops Loodvoet

We had a brief spell back in Rundu and then were back for Ops Loodvoet in March-April. This we initially ran from the army base at Elundu and then Nkongo. It had been a frustrating time for us, having a few companies patrolling in Southern Angola directly to the north of us, during which I had a distinct feeling that the enemy knew exactly what our plans where. We were up against SWAPO Commander Bulanganga's detachment and he turned out to be a very capable guerrilla leader. He ran circles around us and we just did not seem to be able to pin him or his cadres down. They gave us the slip time and again, and on a few occasions mortared our platoons with uncanny, pin-point, accuracy. We lost one white Sergeant and six black troops wounded through a mortar attack while the enemy continued to evade our troops. The Sergeant had the flesh stripped off his legs below the knee by shrapnel. He tragically bled to death before we could casevac him. We had no 'kills' against Commander Bulanganga's troops that time round.

My later analysis of the battalion's radio traffic, messages and codes pointed to the very likely case that they got their intelligence from this source. Prior to any deployment or attack, our radio traffic spiked. All they then had to do was decipher our very basic code system and they would get a wealth of information – even if the really sensitive stuff wasn't sent over the radio. We used this to good effect in our future planning. The number of messages sent on a daily basis was kept constant and most of the information specific to any operation was relayed by courier or through order groups and face-to-face briefings. The East Germans (who I suspected were the ones behind the monitoring of our radio frequencies) would therefore have had little to indicate what we were planning operationally.

Nkongo was a bleak army base but, nonetheless, afforded a time of pleasant *braais* in the evening, sitting round a roaring fire, thick steaks and plenty of Castle Lager … the beer greatly facilitating robust debates as to the realities and virtues of the war we were fighting. Commander Bulanganga was giving us a fine display of guerrilla tactics. A very small number of SWAPO guerrilla fighters were using hit-and-run tactics that tied down a large conventional army in counter-insurgency operations, the South African Defence Force. I was now experiencing first hand, Mao Tse Tung's 'war of the flea'; the father of guerrilla warfare, he likened the guerrillas to a flea biting a dog as by the time the dog (being the conventional army) got to scratch the affected area, the flea was gone … and the dog scratched a far bigger area than had been bitten. In other words, by the time we reacted to the guerrilla action, they more often than not had cut and run, and we had to cover an area far greater than that actually affected. Furthermore, the conventional army's efforts to combat the guerrillas usually resulted in civilians getting caught in the crossfire, encouraging even more of them to turn towards the guerrillas cause. And why were we fighting SWAPO in South West Africa anyway? South Africa was the aggressor, having 'annexed' South West Africa after the Second World War. The guerrillas were doing what I would do if I were in their shoes. Were we somehow fighting for Apartheid back in South Africa? While I didn't quite know what the alternative was, the principle of Apartheid didn't sit too well with me. I knew I had to 'do my bit' as it were so I was comfortable about serving in the Army. So, all in all, there were some complex and sensitive issues here!

As delicate as most of this was at the time, discussing it around the open fire, night after night with copious amounts of beer in the company of my friend, 2nd Lieutenant Heinz Muller, made for some good laughs and fun evenings. Heinz had been lightly wounded a few weeks previously and was assigned to the Tac HQ until ready to rejoin his platoon in the bush. Heinz was an Afrikaans guy of medium height and build, with a fit, athletic air about him. While I reasoned there had to be a smarter way to fight this guerrilla war, he advocated a more direct approach … 'Ons moet vok net voort' ('We must just fuck forward'), meaning we must just attack and keep attacking! The more beer we had, the more entertaining the debate become, and the more Heinz would leap to his feet, eyes blazing, to eloquently re-iterate his grand strategy … *'Ons moet net voort fok!'*

I eventually found most of the answers I was looking for towards the end of the year. However, fate was soon to play its hand because for Heinz and me, the Battle of Savate lay ahead.

9

The Battle of Savate

A signal came through instructing me to report back to our Battalion HQ at the big army base back in Rundu, a few hundred kilometres to the east. We were to begin planning another op, and all the indications were that this was to be a big one. I managed to get a lift in a Puma, this being one of the advantages of being based in the HQ! My mates in the companies were usually trooped around in the back of the huge Kwevoël trucks or in Buffels, exposed to the scorching sun and arriving covered in dust days later.

I wasn't briefed immediately on my return. However, the next few weeks were characterised by UNITA officers and our CSI (Chief Staff Intelligence) spooks hurrying in and out of our intelligence room between meetings with Commandant Ferreira. When the OC finally briefed me so that I could draw up the signals plan, little did I know the significance of what lay ahead.

In what was code named Operation Tiro-Tiro, we were to attack some 400 Angolan army troops (MPLA) in their base at Savate approximately 80km inside Angola on the Cubango River. Our force was to be comprised of three infantry companies, a mortar platoon and our recce wing as stopper groups to the north of the base. Our numbers totalled just some 350 men, which defied the military principle of only attacking if you outnumbered the defenders by three to one. We were to have no artillery or air support as this was to be a covert operation, which we would conduct under the guise of UNITA. UNITA were a guerrilla army operating in Angola and the SADF was supporting them in their fight against the Angolan army troops. The only air support was to be one Puma helicopter for medical casevac purposes, and one Alouette helicopter gunship for an emergency. Any more support of this nature would give the game away as to the fact that we were South African troops and not UNITA. Willem Ratte was to undertake a close target recce with a four-man stick the week leading up to the attack. We were to cross the border into Angola in a convoy of Buffel troop carriers and Kwevoël lorries from the base at Omauni, moving directly north to Savate, and then use the same route out again.

My first step was to request the frequencies to be used on the HF radio networks from Brigade HQ. On being allocated six HF frequencies ranging

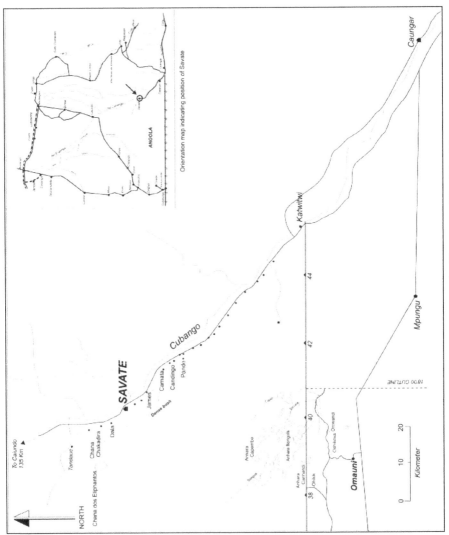

Savate's position in Angola. (Courtesy of Piet Nortje)

from 3 MHz up to 12 MHz, I began the 24-hour testing process between Omauni and Rundu, with a radio check every fifteen minutes. This was the technique I had devised after the total failure of HF communications in the early hours of the aborted attack on the Angolan garrison at Dirico. My suspicions that the enemy were eavesdropping on our radio networks were confirmed while I was doing this testing. The best frequency for use in the early morning turned out to be one that was used by the local doctors as a radio telephone, and one which was monitored closely by the Cubans / East Germans. I had one of them taunt me about the fact that he was listening in; just after I had completed a radio check at about 3.00 am in the morning!! I shudder to think of the information the doctors were unwittingly exposing to the enemy with their daily discussions of medical and other matters.

The HQ contingent took a Puma ride out to Omauni about five days prior to the attack. Final plans and preparations began. The briefing of roughly thirty officers and NCOs was held in the mess hall, a corrugated iron building with a bare concrete floor. I was called on by the OC to present the signals orders and I focused on the frequencies to be used and their associated schedules – as well as warning them not to use HF communications unless absolutely necessary, due to the possibility that their conversations could well be intercepted by the enemy and the transmissions used to get a bearing on our positions. I mentioned my experience a few days earlier with the East German while testing the frequencies and this certainly got their rapt attention!

Lieutenant Willem Ratte, Sergeant Piet van Eeden and Troopers Joao and Casomo, together with a UNITA guide, left in a small convoy of about three Buffels two or three days before the attack was due, to meet up just across the border with a CSI convoy under the command of a 'Senhor Lobb'. The plan was for Senhor Lobb to drop them off 10km north-west of Savate. Willem's team would then carry their folding Klepper canoes (made of a wooden frame covered in canvas) to the river and paddle down that first night to Savate. They would lie up during the day on the eastern bank, positioned on the high ground overlooking the base and then cross over the river each night to reconnoitre the enemy positions. I walked out with them to their armoured Buffels and did final radio checks with them. The big diesels roared into life and they headed up the two track road to the north … they were finally on their way and the assault on Savate had begun.

I had tested and retested the radios they carried to ensure they were working. They had daily radio schedules; times at which they would report

Senhor Lobb with some 'Tiffies' (mechanics).

The infamous Senhor Lobb, who led the convoy astray during the drive into Angola.

back to us. They missed the first 'sched', and my signallers failed to report this to me … I, of course, was responsible for not having checked up on them. I only discovered this when they missed the second 'sched'. We immediately put into action the back-up plan, which was to send a Bosbok spotter plane into the air to try and get comms using direct line of sight, VHF radios. My heart was in my mouth while we waited to hear back from the pilot, fearing the worst and agonising over the fact that we had missed the first radio 'sched'.

To calm my nerves I came up out of the sandbag-covered command bunker and stood on the earthen wall that surrounded the base, quietly looking out over the bush. I allowed my imagination to run away with me as to what might have happened to them … killed, captured, or who knew what else? Maybe if we had been onto it at the first missed radio schedule it would have been different … I laid it on for myself pretty thick! It wasn't too long before the signaller's head popped out from the sunken door of the command bunker to tell me that the pilot had made contact with them. It later transpired that their HF radio had got wet in the river crossings, which explained the breakdown in communication. It was with huge relief I learned that all was well with them.

Willem Ratte later told me that their UNITA guide, Senhor Lobb, had dropped them off immediately west of Savate instead of 10km to the northwest. When they had walked east towards the river, they were actually walking directly towards the base at Savate. Hearing vehicles ahead of them and thinking they were north of Savate, they skirted round to the south to get to the river. As the sun was setting, they assembled their two Klepper canoes and cautiously paddled for about 8km downriver, thinking they were heading towards Savate, when in actual fact they were going away from the base! They only realised their mistake when they came to a deserted town just before midnight and their guide identified it as a place marked on Willem's old Portuguese road map which was actually below Savate. Willem and his team then paddled furiously back upstream for the remainder of the night in order to get back into position opposite Savate before the sun rose. This was no mean feat, especially as they had to negotiate a set of rapids in the process. As such, they lost the opportunity to recce Savate on the first night.

As the sun rose they were close to Savate but still a distance away. Exhausted, they lay up on the eastern bank of the river for the day. They eventually made it to Savate the next evening. They left their kit on the eastern side of the river again, opposite the base, and Willem and Sergeant Piet van Eeden went across and did their initial reconnaissance. Their primary objective set by Ferreira was to confirm that the enemy were still occupying the base and to obtain a rough estimate of their numbers. That the enemy were still in the base soon became very evident. In fact, it became increasingly obvious to Willem that there was far more activity in and around the base than that which could be ascribed to 400 troops. Ferreira mulled over calling off the attack, but without a firm estimate of how many troops there actually were, he decided to continue the planned operation anyway. After the attack, it transpired that there were over 1,000 enemy in the base. Had UNITA deliberately misled us by telling us that there were only 400? Had they misled us to ensure we saw the attack through?!

At long last the main convoy was ready to leave Omauni for the two-day journey to Savate. In the command Buffel were Commandant Ferreira, Captain Erasmus the Intelligence Officer, myself the Signals Officer, Sergeant Major Ueckerman the RSM, Lance Corporal Bruce Anders as my signaller and an Ops Clerk we nicknamed 'Lappies' (Rags). Staff-Sergeant Ron Gregory manned the Browning machine-gun mounted at the front of the Buffel. My good friend 2nd Lieutenant Tim Patrick and Corporal John van Dyk, both from the HQ intelligence unit and who reported to Captain Erasmus, were assigned to the companies as intelligence liaison. Having been confined to HQ duties since their arrival on the border, the significance of their inexperience

The journey in: cheerful troops in the back of a Kwevoël, with Buffels in the background.

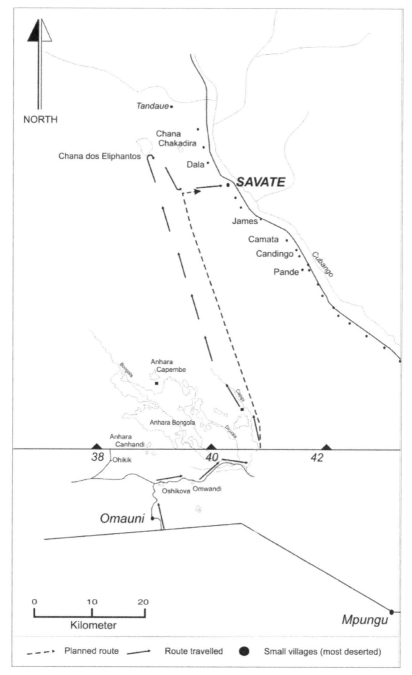

Savate – the route travelled by the convoy from Omauni, getting lost and finding ourselves
at Chana dos Elfantos, whereafter the Bosbok spotter plane was called up to got us
back on track to get to the point at which we would continue on foot. Using the aircraft
posed a serious risk of compromising ourselves to the enemy. (Courtesy of Piet Nortje)

only dawned on me after the battle. We crossed over the border and spent the first night in Angola, arriving at the 'set-off' point at the end of the second day.

Those two days in the Buffel seemed like an eternal lifetime. Strapped into our seats in case we hit a land mine, we sat back-to-back facing outwards, five seats abreast, with the incessant sun pounding down on us. As incredible as these vehicles were in terms of their ruggedness, no one had thought to design a cover to shield the occupants from the sun. To this was added the relentless swaying and bucking of the Buffel as it ground its way along the twisting, sandy track, constantly throwing us against our shoulder straps and the kit piled up at the back of the armoured compartment which kept falling on us. Tempers became frayed and our patience with each other was stretched to the limit.

And to add to the tension in the command vehicle, the convoy got lost on the second day, compliments of the same UNITA guide, Senhor Lobb, who had dropped Willem Ratte at the wrong location a few days earlier. We had to call in the Bosbok spotter plane to get us back on track. This caused some consternation in the HQ as it may well have compromised the attack by alerting the enemy to South African activity in the area. With the Bosbok flying directly above us, Commandant Ferreira was unable to speak to the pilot using the ground-to-air VHF radio. With the ever-present experience of failed communications at Dirico lurking in his mind, he uttered a few choice expletives and hurled the handset at me. Fortunately for me it came to the end of its tether just inches from my face before bouncing back. The pilot disappeared back south again, returning a few hours later and this time we could speak to him clearly. To my satisfaction, it turned out that it had been the radio in *his* aircraft that was faulty and not mine. I was then able to appreciate the comical side of Ferreira's outburst, especially after his sheepish apology.

By the end of the second day, we had arrived at the point at which we would leave the vehicles and begin the overnight march to the various positions, from which each section would launch their attack. The HQ element had a platoon of infantry attached under the command of 2nd Lieutenant 'Trompie' Theron to guard it. We would be coming in behind Alpha Company commanded by Lieutenant Charl Muller, with Lieutenant Jim Ross and his Foxtrot Company to our right. Charl was the Adjutant of the Battalion and was commanding Captain Tony Nienaber's Alpha Company as Tony was away on a course. Capt Sam Heap's Charlie Company would attack the base from the north of the airfield.

Troops resting before the long night march toward Savate.

As the sun set, the OC held his confirmatory and final Orders Group with the HQ element, the three company commanders and the mortar platoon commander. We sat on the sand amongst the tufts of grass alongside the two-track road and he asked each of us to touch on the final pertinent points ... logistics – Major Louw; intelligence – Capt Erasmus; and signals – myself. The key issue discussed was the possibility of that there were many more enemy troops than expected ... yet even given this possibility, it was decided not to change the battle plan. As he summed up the latest intelligence assessment and got the opinions of the company commanders, I couldn't help thinking that Lieutenants Charl Muller and Jim Ross certainly looked the part. To their camouflaged battle fatigues, AK-47 rifles and blacked out faces they had added their own style of headgear. Jim Ross had a dirty cloth tied over his head and knotted at the back. He was the quintessential bush fighter ... still, dark, disturbing eyes and of medium height, with a squat strong physique and an aggressive temperament. Charl Muller had a dark coloured bandana tied around his head tennis player style ... a lean, suave, good looking guy with a very pretty young wife back in Rundu. It was the last time I was to see him alive.

The other company commander sitting in the circle was Sam Heap. Sam was a huge guy with a hand that dwarfed mine in a handshake and a friendly demeanour that was ever ready with a broad smile. Looking around, I was pleased to be on their side in the upcoming fight. I couldn't help thinking that it would have been good to have had Tony Nienaber with us as well … a very level-headed, dependable guy with a quiet, yet authoritative air about him.

The long night began. Everyone had just their light, first-line kit on – chest webbing with spare magazines, one day's water and rations, grenades affixed to belts – leaving their Machillas (H frame rucksack) in the Buffels. Except for the mortar platoon, who were shouldering their heavy base plates and 81mm mortar tubes, all the troops were in first-line order. The heavy 81mm mortar bombs were initially distributed amongst all the troops, but these poor mortar buggers had to then carry the whole lot, later on in the night, the last few kilometres to their fire positions. My signaller, Lance Corporal Bruce Anders, and I were in a similar situation. In addition to our first-line kit, he and I took turns to carry the Machilla with the big HF radio, the spare Nicad batteries, handsets and everything else I thought anyone might need. All this equipment was so heavy, that to put the rucksack on we had to prop it up against a tree, thread our arms through the straps and then roll over onto our stomachs before pushing ourselves up off the sand. We then completed this complicated manoeuvre by using the tree to pull ourselves upright. We certainly had our work cut out for us that night! And Bruce was not a big guy either. Of medium height, wiry and very fit, he had been recommended to me by Willem Ratte. As an Ops Clerk back in the base at Omauni, he had seen limited time in the bush and certainly had no combat experience. He was to acquit himself well over the next few days.

We were following a two-track, sand road that led to the base. By mid-evening we had entered a thickly wooded area with tall trees that soared above us, blacking out the night sky. Through the darkness that enveloped us, we heard a heavy vehicle grinding its way towards us, and I could soon see its lights weaving through the trees. Ferreira gave the quick battle orders for only one squad to open fire on the vehicle with strict instructions to conserve ammunition. In the silence that followed the brief burst of rifle fire, we heard the left cab door crack open and someone fall out onto the grass alongside the track. He crawled off into the undergrowth and was left to his own devices, most likely to die of his wounds. As we passed the Gaz truck, I could see a dark shape on the right hand side of the cab and could smell the strong, sickly sweet smell of blood. Being left-hand-drive and with right-hand-drive vehicles back

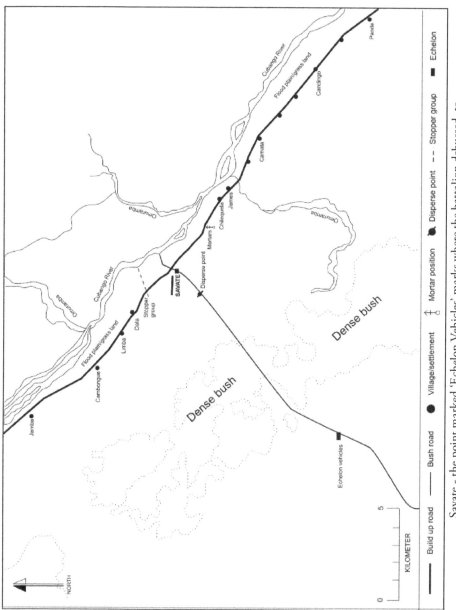

Savate – the point marked 'Echelon Vehicles' marks where the battalion debussed, to walk through the night to the dispersal point. (Courtesy of Piet Nortje)

home, it was the passenger on the right-hand side and not the driver that had been shot to pieces.

By the early hours of the morning we had reached the edge of the thick forest, the point from which everyone was to split up and head for their allotted kick-off points, Sam Heap to the north and the mortar platoon to the south near the river. While we moved up past some troops who had pulled over to the side of the road to let us through, I heard my friend Heinz Muller quietly call out my name in the darkness

"Justin!?"

"Heinz … .. ?"

"Jy moet lekker wees…"

Before I could answer we were gone. His tone of voice sent a chill down my spine … it was as if he was trying to tell me something. Translated literally it means "you must be well", but it can come to mean many things depending on the tone of voice and context within which it is verbalised; from a warning to watch your step, to being encouraged to look out for yourself, or just to have fun. As I struggled along under the heavy Machilla, I thought about his comment. What puzzled me was that he seemed to be telling me to "go well" as a form of farewell. I was to have my answer during a lull in the battle ahead.

By about 2am we had reached the point from which the companies in front of us would launch the attack. The HQ element stopped under some tall trees, which stood alongside a two-track sand road that ran from the base in a southerly direction. The pale moonlight allowed us to see clearly enough, and everyone immediately fell asleep where they sat down. I went through my usual drill of setting up comms with the Tac HQ back in Omauni. Instead of slanting the wire antenna as I usually did to maximise the range, I threw the weight (an outer casing of a grenade to which the wire was attached) straight up into the tall tree above me. I was very surprised to get crystal clear communication back to Omauni some 80km away – very unusual for that time of night as it must have been about two o'clock in the morning. I soon fell asleep along with everyone else. A little later I found that I had woken myself up by having answered a radio call from Omauni, speaking to them while still asleep. Commandant Ferreira gave me a strange look before he too fell asleep again.

The sun had just risen and we were supposed to have already initiated the attack. We had been hampered by the thick forest behind us and as a result, Sam Heap's company and the 81mm mortar guys were behind schedule. I

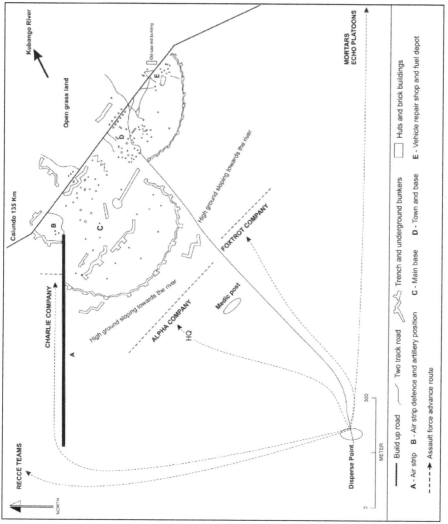

Savate – from the dispersal point marking the positions to begin the attack. (Courtesy of Piet Nortje)

Final briefing: Cmdt Ferreira (seated right) briefing company and
platoon commanders with faces already painted with 'black-is-beautiful'.
Kwevoël and Buffel troop transports are in the background.

stood up to watch Sam Heap's Charlie Company file silently passed us to skirt
to the west of the base in order to come around and attack from the north.
They looked like the formidable lot that they were, quietly and purposefully
filing past with their rifles held comfortably at the ready across their chests …
our distinctive style. Someone waved, it could have been Sam Heap or John
van Dyk but I couldn't recognise them … they all looked the same in their
'black-is-beautiful' so I couldn't distinguish any of the white guys from the
troops.

They all wore our external ops cammo uniforms and the Portuguese-
style army caps along with the distinct 32 Battalion brown leather boots with
canvas sides and flat rubber soles. To this was added their first-line kit with its
chest webbing, basic medical kit and hand-grenade pouches. They carried an
assortment of weapons including AK-47s and R1s with the odd pistol as back-
up; light machine-guns such as Russian RPKs, RPDs and PKMs were carried
along with FN NATO MAGs, the glistening 7.62mm ammunition belts
draped over their shoulders. Support weapons included 60mm commando

mortar pipes, ubiquitous Russian RPG rocket launchers with spare rockets tied untidily across their shoulders and the odd *Snot-neuse* (Afrikaans for snot-nose), a robust and dependable American grenade launcher. Bayonets were affixed to their web belts and extra grenades (fragmentation and phosphorous) were carried where there was space. Most troops had 60mm mortar bombs hanging off their webbing ready to pass along to the mortar guys when the fight started.

The officers and NCOs had VHF radios attached to their web belts, as part of their first-line kit, with the telltale blade antenna sticking up behind their armpits. They usually folded these in half with some black tape so they wouldn't rattle or stick up conspicuously high. I could see the practicality behind this, but it certainly gave me grey hairs as it significantly affected the radio's transmission range. No comms or bad comms was my responsibility, even given these idiosyncrasies. They were behind schedule and we still had a way to go. Watching this lot file past, I could understand why the Angolan Army referred to us as 'Os Terreveis' … 'The Terrible Ones' … we certainly looked the part.

What also stuck in my mind was the quiet, steady, assurance of the way they moved, even now that things weren't going as expected. Having planned to attack at dawn, we were well behind schedule and we knew that we were up against greater odds than initially anticipated. Willem Ratte and his team had lost a valuable day for reconnaissance as they had been dropped off in the wrong position. As such, they hadn't had time to carry out the detailed observation of the enemy base they had planned. After his initial reports of more activity in the base than that of the number of enemy troops estimated, Willem confirmed that there was significant activity on both sides of the airfield, with a notable number of enemy on the northern side of the airfield … against which we were sending only two platoons of Sam Heap's Charlie Company. The other two companies, Alpha and Foxtrot, led by Jim Ross and Charl Muller, attacking from the south ahead of us in the HQ, had a wider area to cover. Even given Willem's report of the greater than expected movement on the northern side, Ferreira could not be sure as to whether this was routine base activity or whether there were actually more troops present than anticipated. Hence, and as a result, he kept the plan unchanged.

Normal South African army attacks had all the conventional support of pre-emptive heavy artillery bombardments and air strikes, with the troops assaulting the enemy positions in armoured vehicles. We had none of that.

This was to be the simplest and most basic of infantry attacks. Supported by a brief 81mm mortar bombardment that would only be effective if it caught the enemy out of their trenches, our troops would then attack the entrenched positions head-on with each soldier three metres apart and line abreast … the way UNITA guerrillas would do it. No surprise there, as it was UNITA who we were supposed to be emulating. Ferreira's supreme confidence in his troops had him flout the basic military principle of only attacking if you outnumbered the enemy 3:1. We were not even 1:1 as there were only 350 of us against an initial combat estimate of some 400 enemy. And we now knew we were up against considerably more than that, and we were about to attack in broad daylight. Completely outnumbered and against the odds, we were committed to the assault. Commandant Ferreira was with us, not sitting safely back in a Tactical HQ somewhere. We trusted his judgement and leadership explicitly. There was a steady, measured confidence that settled amongst us. There was absolutely no doubt, no hesitation in any of our minds, about the task ahead.

Not long after the sun had risen, Sam Heap confirmed that Charlie Company was in position to the north. But the 81mm mortar guys were seriously behind schedule, having been hampered by even thicker bush down by the river where they had struggled to get into position. To this was added the heavy mortar tubes, base plates and all the big 81 mm mortar bombs they were burdened with. They also had great difficulty trying to communicate through the dense bush on their short-range VHF radio sets. Sergeant Piet van Eeden and the UNITA guide from Willem Ratte's recce team were waiting to guide them in to their position – yet couldn't get comms with them. As dawn approached, the two of them had to withdraw sharply to their Observation Post across the river. This left the mortar guys to find their own firing point, after which they still had to set up their base plates and tubes before commencing their fire mission. Whilst we waited, the sun continued to rise.

A message came through to us that there were three young boys walking up the road towards us. Ferreira's orders were to bayonet them should they try to run back, but leave them should they continue to walk away from the FAPLA base. I sat there with my heart in my mouth, quietly willing them not to turn around. As they drew level to where we were sitting, one of them looked over to his right and suddenly saw me sitting there, deathly still and just a few metres away in the tall grass. As our eyes met, he visibly caught his breath and his eyes flew wide open, absolute terror etched across his face. I must have looked like the devil incarnate; armed to the teeth and dressed in my filthy camouflaged uniform, adorned with 'black-is-beautiful' camouflage paint streaking from the sweat on my face. Mesmerised, they stiffly kept on walking … away from the base. Once past us, they could contain themselves no longer and broke into a chaotic sprint down the sandy road, elbows pumping wildly and the pink under-soles of their bare feet flashing up nearly as high as their shoulder blades … boy, could those little fuckers run!!

It was only at about ten o'clock that our mortars finally swung into action. We heard the low, muffled cough of the bombs leaving the tubes off to our right, followed by the "ka-boom … ka-boom" as they began landing in the base ahead of us. The waiting was finally over … this was it. We followed the thin line of Alpha Company's troops stretched out to our left and right, a couple of hundred metres ahead of us – with Foxtrot off to our right – advancing towards the sound of the crashing mortars. The base was so spread out that I couldn't be sure what effect the mortars had, other than to chase the enemy into their trenches. Looking to either side of me I could see the black, battle-hardened troops from Lieutenant Trompie's platoon assigned to us as 'HQ protection'. They were walking steadily forward, three metres apart and line abreast. There were no other troops in the world I would rather have had at

Part of the bunker system.

Sleeping quarters.

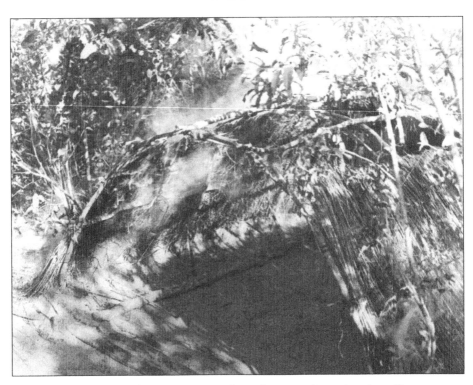

Temporary sleeping quarters to keep the sun and morning dew off.

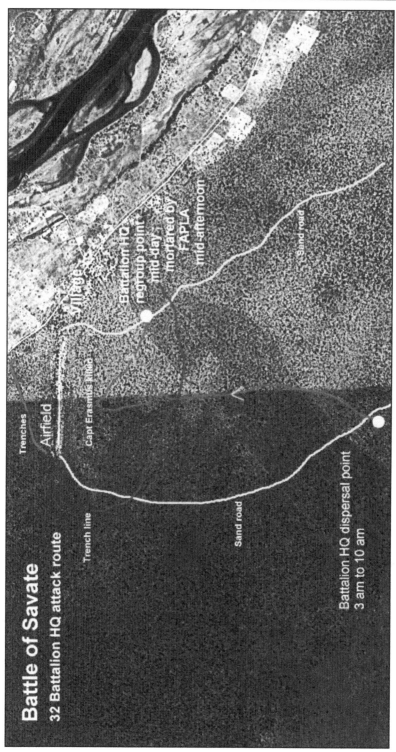

Battle of Savate

32 Battalion HQ attack route

Trenches

Airfield

Trench line

Capt Erasmus killed

Sand road

Battalion HQ dispersal point
3 am to 10 am

Village

Battalion HQ
regroup point
mid-day

mortared by
FAPLA
mid-afternoon

Sand road

The route followed by the HQ element from the beginning of the attack to the mid-afternoon mortar attack.

my side. The HQ moved forward in a loose group formation, Commandant Ferreira, Captain Erasmus, Sergeant-Major Ueckerman, myself, 'Lappies' the Ops Clerk and my signaller, Bruce Anders.

The terrain was very open, with scraggly three metre high trees scattered amongst the odd tuft of grass. The ubiquitous white sand kept tugging at the heels of my boots as I shuffled forward under the weight of the dreaded Machilla. The terrain rose gently ahead of us, before gently sloping down to the airfield that lay about 2km ahead. With the airfield just ahead in the middle of the base somewhere, Alpha Company were directly to our front, Foxtrot Company just off to our right, the river about 3km further on, whilst the mortar platoon was about 3km to our right and slightly behind us. The medevac post was to our rear and the logistics guys were just a little further back with all the vehicles and supplies.

A few minutes later an almighty roar erupted ahead of us as the companies came up against the trenches. We soon began hearing the angry buzz of rifle bullets as they neared the end of their trajectory, zipping viciously between us and someone decided that it would be sensible to take cover by lying flat on the sand. I lay there, already exhausted from almost no sleep the night before and from carrying the dreaded Machilla, wondering how I would ever explain the sound ahead of me. Nearly two thousand automatic rifles and machine guns were firing together, punctuated by the boom of exploding mortar bombs and RPG rockets, all of which filled the air around us whilst hammering our eardrums, numbing our brains and seemingly drilling down into our chests. The best analogy I can think of was that the gunfire sounded as if we were in a confined space with countless marbles beating furiously and continuously against a tin roof above our heads ... a hailstorm gone mad. The ferociousness of the enemy's response immediately struck a chord in us all ... while we had always known that we would be outnumbered, the full extent of by how much began to dawn on us. However, there was nothing to be done, no alternative, but to follow through what we had begun.

Not long after the attack commenced, the whole sky from horizon to horizon suddenly filled with the roar of what seemed to be swarms of fighter jets shrieking over our heads. This was followed by a tremendous explosion a few kilometres behind us with a sound that rattled our teeth. One of the older hands muttered *Monakashita* ('Stalin organs' or 'Red-eye rockets') ... it certainly frightened the living daylights out of us even though it went well over our heads. It must have scared the shit out of the mortar guys in whose vicinity

One of the many enemy dead.

Some of the huts in the base with trenches in the foreground.

the rockets were exploding. Not being very accurate and firing only a single rocket at a time, they did not have much success except for having a dramatic psychological effect. At this point someone wisely realised that lying prone wasn't achieving much and the order to advance was given again. I struggled up off the sand and laboured forward under the accursed and heavy rucksack.

No sooner had we begun to make our advance on the base again, when I heard the unmistakeably rapid beat of rotor blades and the whining turbines of a large helicopter approaching low, hard and fast … my blood froze. "Hind gunship!" someone called out and we scurried for suitable cover, but there was none. I feared these deadly helicopters more than anything, having heard a story of how one such aircraft had reportedly decimated a platoon of ours soon after the '75 Angolan war of independence. Its armour protection and chin-mounted cannon linked to the pilot's helmet sight made it a deadly machine. Darting from pathetic tree to pathetic tree for cover, we must have looked like rats caught in a barn when the lights are suddenly switched on. The helicopter roared over us at tree top height and it was with huge relief that we saw it was one of our big Pumas. But what the hell was it doing here? We were hugely concerned as it had flown straight over the FAPLA army base and the raging battle ahead of us. It seemed the pilot had overshot the rear echelon group where he was to wait in order to casevac the wounded. He must have suddenly seen the airfield in the middle of the base, and realising where he was, turned the aircraft practically on the spot and shot out of there like a bat out of hell. A friend of mine, Lance Corporal Grant Larkin, who was an ops medic on board the helicopter, later told me that he was scared shitless they would take rounds up through the floor of the aircraft and he sat there helplessly praying one wouldn't be for him!

The sound of the bullets had now changed to that distinct, deadly 'whip-crack' as they passed between us, and I knew we were now close. Unbeknown to us at the time, Alpha Company up ahead had advanced into a fire-storm, taking heavy casualties and they were soon to lose their Company Commander, Charl Muller and their Intelligence Officer, Tim Patrick … and we too were about to get drawn into the tail end of it. Trompie's troops a few metres ahead of us started firing while moving steadily forward, but I couldn't see anything. Astonished, I realised that the trenches were but five metres ahead. They were an ingenious design, a metre wide and deep enough for a man to stand in with his head and shoulders sticking out. They zigzagged off to our left and right, not running straight for more than three metres. What made them almost invisible, until you were on top of them, was that they had no protective mound in front of them, but rather were flush with the ground. As we were soon to learn, they were difficult to clear unless you systematically worked down the trench line. The companies ahead of us had advanced over the trenches to get into the base, as we were about to do. I peered into the three-metre section in front of me, and seeing nothing down there, backed up and took a running jump to clear it.

We hadn't moved thirty metres into the base area when we started taking fire from behind us … the enemy were still in the trenches!! Everyone around me dived to the ground. With the weight of the Machilla on my back I was a lot slower, carefully kneeling to put my hand out in front of me and lower myself to the ground when I was suddenly pitched face forward into the sand. Thinking at the time it was the weight of the backpack, I later saw that a bullet had passed through the Machilla, missing my neck by a few centimetres. Being the only one carrying a rucksack that stood nearly as high as the top of my head, I must have stuck out like a sore thumb, making an obvious and inviting target. Trompie's troops immediately engaged the enemy behind us. I rolled onto my side and pulled my arms free of the Machilla. I had had more than enough of carrying it, and I shouted to Bruce Anders to take over. He was clearly not happy at the prospect, but, fuck it, it was his turn anyway … and rank in this instance had its privileges!

Finally free of the burdensome pack, I was now ready to actively participate in the fight. I suddenly and inexplicably felt incredibly alive, aware of every sense in my body … as if on a high. I wasn't tired any more, I felt fitter, stronger. I could see clearer with all colours being really vivid, my sense of touch was enhanced and my hearing sharper. I can only think that it must have been the adrenaline pumping through my veins that was channelling my fear into a positive survival mode, or maybe our training ensured this reaction and not the debilitating stomach-churning butterflies that was the alternative.

Seeing some huts off to our right, Captain Erasmus and I moved to clear them. I fired a few rounds through the wooden-poled wall of one hut while Erasmus did the same for another. Sticking my head through the door, I saw that it was empty. Erasmus screamed out "watch your back, watch your back!!" as we took fire from back up towards the trench line. I emptied my magazine in that direction, which only served to draw more fire. I changed magazines, pulling a fresh one from my chest webbing and throwing the empty down my shirt front. "Watch your back, watch your back!!" Erasmus screamed again as

Enemy captured at Savate.

we took fire from the direction of the river. It suddenly dawned on me that he and I were alone, as the HQ group had moved on down towards the airstrip. I kept turning to face incoming rounds, not seeing clearly who was firing at us. Erasmus and I were spinning back-to-back, jabbering and shouting warnings to each other, moving in the direction we thought the HQ had gone. I couldn't help thinking how comical it must have looked, two HQ officers clearly out of their depth, in the shit, in the midst of a raging firefight. The thought, "I can't fucking believe I've got myself into this!" going round and round in my mind. From the huts to getting back to the HQ group is a blur… I simply can't remember. How we found them I don't know, and when we got there, I had two or three empty magazines clonking around in my shirtfront. I hadn't had time to put them back into my chest webbing.

The OC had some sharp words to say to me about being separated from him as I was carrying one of the VHF radios he needed in order for him to access part of his command net. Little did he realise just how pleased I was to be back with the platoon and the extent to which he was speaking to the converted!

Trompie's HQ defence platoon was strung out expectantly in a skirmish

Enemy captured at Savate.

line running down the slope, facing towards the river. No sooner had we arrived when all hell broke loose around us. Unencumbered by the heavy Machilla, I dived with alacrity onto the sand. I fired off half a magazine between the two man MAG machine-gun crew a few metres to my left and Captain Erasmus in a clump of grass on my right, before crawling forward into the firing line. It was very comforting to hear the roar of the controlled bursts of machine-gun fire from the MAG to my left ... and it was good to be back with the platoon. Running the risk of losing the initiative if we stayed stationary, I shouted through the maelstrom of gunfire to advance. The MAG gunners began gathering their glistening ammunition belts, draping them over their shoulders and preparing to hoist up the gun. Changing to my last magazine as I got up, I realised there was no response from Erasmus. "Captain, Captain ... we have to advance, we have to advance" ... no response again. Bruce Anders was shouting something behind me, and I realised he was telling me that there appeared to be something wrong with him.

I reversed back from the firing line, and crawled round alongside him in the grass. To my horror, I saw he had a hideous throat wound with blood gushing from his mouth as he struggled to breathe. Something snapped in me, and jumping up I ran down the skirmish line screaming for the medic. Thirty metres down the slope, I saw Sergeant Major Ueckerman on all fours crawling up towards me ... an unusual posture for this big, burly Regimental Sergeant Major, with his red handle bar moustache and bellowing voice that struck the fear of God into all around him on the parade ground. He reached up and pulled me down by my chest webbing as I was about to run past him, still shouting for the medic.

"*Looty, wats fout?*" (Lieutenant, what's wrong?)

Not making much sense at first, I took a deep breath and told him about Captain Erasmus and that he needed a medic, in fact, he needed a doctor, fast.

"The medics are all busy *Looty*, and so are all the doctors ... there's nothing we can do right now."

"FUCK IT ... ... !" Numbly I began crawling back up to Erasmus. I looked behind my shoulder and to my amazement I saw Commandant Ferreira strolling up the firing line with his AK-47 slung casually by its strap off his shoulder. He had two VHF radios strapped to his web belt and he was listening intently, an ear-piece pressed to each ear. He was completely oblivious to the firefight raging round him, and while the rest of us were slithering around like lizards; he looked every bit as if he was out on a Sunday afternoon stroll. The advance had faltered on my side of the line when I had gone apeshit looking for a medic. I lay miserably in the grass next to Captain Erasmus as the fight continued. His left arm was thrust forward, twisted crookedly above the elbow. I watched helplessly as he slowly died, his gaping neck wound causing him to gulp for air as blood gushed from his mouth each time he tried to breath. Medically there was nothing I could do as this was way past my basic combat first aid skills. In fact I don't think anyone could have done anything for him. His face slowly lowered towards the sand until his shoulders gently heaved for the last time. Helplessly, all I could do was stick with him and keep him covered, firing only when I had to, trying to conserve the last of my ammunition ... it was possibly the longest, loneliest twenty minutes of my life.

The firefight slowly died down and I got up when I saw the OC standing behind me, still talking intently on his radio command network. Hoisting the Machilla up against a tree, I plugged a whip antenna into the big HF radio and switched it on in case the OC needed it. When I tried testing comms, I got a strange "bbbrrrrr" in the earpiece. Lifting the HF radio up, I saw a bullet hole through it. Inspecting the rucksack, I could see the neat entry hole at the back and the jagged exit. I realised with a chill that had I not leaned forward to lie flat when the enemy opened fire from the trenches behind us at the beginning of the battle, the bullet would have hit me in the back of my neck.

I heard the OC mention my friend Tim Patrick a few times over the radio. When he finished, I asked him if Tim was OK. "He's dead", he said quietly. An empty, numb, cold feeling settled in me and I turned and punched the tree next to me, which turned out to be a dumb thing to do as the bark was rough. Fuck ... my hand hurt! At least it gave me something else to think about for a while. He had been burnt to death by a phosphorous grenade.

By now it was just past midday, and the battle had begun to die down. Reports started coming in from the various companies. Alpha and Foxtrot had taken the base to the south of the airfield as well as the few buildings that made up the village at the southern end of the runway; Sam Heap's Charlie Company, which had hit the base to the north of the airstrip, had retreated in the face of overwhelming firepower, most notably from a 14.5mm anti-aircraft gun. They had come back round to our side of the base. And then my friend Heinz Muller's name came in as one of those killed. He had taken three machine gun bullets to his stomach, and died an hour later ... . I sat down next to the Machilla with my back against the tree, rifle across my lap with that empty cold feeling settling in my stomach again. I looked numbly up into the beautiful blue of the sky and took a deep breath … *"Justin, jy moet lekker wees"* ("Justin, you must go well") echoed in my mind. Now it made sense. He had been saying goodbye and had been wishing me well. "FUCK IT! … . *FUCK IT!*" I said quietly as my emotions welled up. A deep sense of helplessness threatened to overwhelm me.

We began gathering ourselves together to regroup on the side of the base closest to the river. Bruce Anders suggested it was now time to abandon the heavy Machilla, with the now unserviceable HF radio, which had proved such a burden during the battle. When we had come under fire just before Captain Erasmus was shot and he had dived for cover, the heavy rucksack had pinned him face down. So much so that he couldn't even lift his head. In his attempts to extricate himself, it caused him to roll onto his side, almost like a tortoise on its back with its legs flailing in the air. As he struggled to free his arms from the straps with bullets cracking past his ears, he was convinced they were to be his last moments. I could understand his aversion to the rucksack but I insisted he pick it up. He later told me the only reason he did what he was told to do was that, from the look in my eyes, he was convinced I was going to shoot him on the spot for insubordination!

As we were about to move off to regroup, I noticed a young FAPLA soldier who had been brought in by the troops. Lying propped up on one elbow, he looked up at us with a beautiful trusting smile, flashing white teeth against his boyish black face. His foot had been shot off just above his boot, and it was hanging loosely by some skin. Surprisingly, there was very little blood. I remember feeling unreasonably pissed off with him and at first, thinking "you might have no foot but at least you are alive you miserable fuck".

"What do we do with this guy?" I asked, as we were about to move off …"Shoot him" came the reply. "Jesus Christ!!" I muttered quietly to myself. Stunned at this directive, I saw he was still smiling anxiously and his eyes were darting furtively between us, not understanding what we were saying, confused as to who we were and desperately seeking empathy. Shoot him? I couldn't do it. I turned to Lappies who stood next to me. Seeing the look in my eyes and before I could say anything, he exploded *"Nee vok!"* ("No fuck!")… his contemptuous attitude for once working in his favour. I then noticed one of our black troops step forward and, miserably, I turned my back and began to walk away.

Following the OC and his group, I turned to see the troop dispatch the wounded FAPLA soldier. Being a battle-hardened veteran, I was surprised to see how he had to brace himself. Standing over him he placed his legs apart and with his rifle pulled firmly into his shoulder, he fired three rounds into him. I guess the young FAPLA troop had got up too close to us and the risk of him surviving, to tell the tale of strange white men with blacked-out faces, was just too great. Being in the middle of the battle we couldn't get him back to any medical assistance anyhow. His youthful face, with the beautiful trusting smile, desperately seeking empathy from us, haunts me to this day.

Walking towards the river and the reorganisation area I saw a small tongue of flame licking at a patch of grass, and wondered if that was where Tim Patrick had died. A little further on we came across the massive mobile pontoon bridge which finally explained the tank tracks we had seen in the aerial photos, and which had caused such consternation and debate in the planning phase ... tanks ... the mere thought of them had struck the fear of God in me! If I had come up against one, my plan was simply to run like hell! They were parked in an area that appeared to be a field workshop as there were some vehicles scattered around in various states of repair. One of the platoon commanders later showed me the mark on the top of his cap, which had been shot off his head by a FAPLA soldier hiding behind one of these vehicles. He had then managed to kill him, shooting him in the head as he peered round a wheel ... it had been a close call! We moved on past one of our massive Kwevoël lorries

Soviet mobile pontoon bridge.

parked under some protective trees. It had an armoured cab and a large flatbed at the back. They were loading our dead onto it and the body bags pretty much covered the entire flatbed.

We came to the high ground that looked down onto the floodplains leading to the river and met up with a handful of Buffels that had come down to resupply us. I thankfully reloaded my magazines with fresh rounds. We were straddling a small two-track road that ran down into the tiny village that was between the airfield and the river, and through which the main north-south road ran. There was a steep bank between us and the main road.

I was between the Buffels and the bank when a black troop asked me what to do with a FAPLA soldier he had with him. He was a well-built, fatherly looking guy with a horrendous wound on the side of his neck. It had splayed open revealing raw, matted flesh. I did a double take as I had assumed he was one of ours. Both Three-Two and FAPLA were wearing camouflage battle fatigues that looked very similar – it was difficult to tell the difference until you got close up, and it was this that had caused so much confusion in the early parts of the battle. Before I could answer him, and right on cue, a mortar bomb crashed down a few metres away. The troop dived for cover and I instinctively ducked. I turned to see the FAPLA soldier making good his escape and was bringing my rifle up to bear when another mortar bomb landed about 30 metres away. Self-preservation taking priority, I turned and instinctively ran for the Buffels. I last saw the prisoner disappearing down the bank towards the river.

The mortar bombs began to crash down amongst us in earnest. The Buffel drivers had decided that discretion was the better part of valour and were returning to the holding area behind us with a great deal of alacrity. I was running towards them in a half crouch, flinching with each explosion, undecided and unsure as to what was going on as the Buffels bucked and roared back up the track. As if in slow motion, I saw one of the drivers through the armoured glass panel on either side of his head. As he drew level with me a mortar bomb exploded just the other side of the Buffel. The armoured glass on the far side of his head starred instantly into a myriad of spider webs as shrapnel smashed into it. Spurred on anew, with the big diesel bellowing, he careened off up the sand track with the armoured vehicle swaying and bouncing around like a bull gone mad.

With nowhere to run to, I turned and headed back to where I had started and saw the OC walking towards me. I dived onto the sand and crawled into a small indent under a scraggly bush, thrusting my rifle foreword. Not being able to see anyone else around, the OC joined me to peer through our meagre cover, not sure what to expect. Were the enemy just trying to hammer us or was this the precursor to an infantry counter-attack? Some of the bombs were hitting the branches of the trees above and shrapnel whizzed menacingly down into the sand around us. The mortar barrage was reaching its crescendo when one exploded just a few metres in front of us and chunks of shrapnel smashed through the bush, just inches above our heads. The OC wriggled closer, trying to share my measly indent for cover. I moved half out to make room, not that it gave us much protection. It was the first time I had seen him show any concern for his own safety.

He immediately started speaking on his command net again. I heard the mortar platoon commander ask if he should use the new phosphorous mortar bombs in retaliation. Fresh from the research factory back in South Africa, it was the first time we had taken them into combat. Being the humane person he was, he was reluctant to use these as they would inflict terrible wounds. On impacting the ground, these bombs would explode and disperse a cloud of deadly phosphorous to a radius of about thirty metres. Phosphorous burns when exposed to oxygen, making it almost impossible to extinguish if it lands on you. He hesitated and seemed to reflect on the day's events, before steeling himself and giving the command to open fire with them.

With the mortar duel gaining tempo, Commandant Ferreira and I lay beneath our pathetic cover. I had my left forearm out in front of me with my rifle resting on it to keep it out of the sand. Mortar bombs continued to crash around us and with not much else to do but wait for whatever, I rested my cheek against the stock of my rifle and fell into an exhausted sleep. I woke up hearing "Justin! Justin!" as Ferreira elbowed me urgently. When he saw that I was merely asleep and not dead, he said with relief and humour in his eyes "It's a terrible war, isn't it!?" I grunted a reply and fell asleep again with the mortars still smashing down, seeking us out amongst the trees.

Unbeknown to us, Ferreira and I were almost alone. The Buffels had all dashed back out of range of the mortars and most of Alpha and Foxtrot companies' troops had melted back towards the rear echelon vehicles, to escape the mortar bombardment. Having survived the madness of the earlier assault, they had had enough. On getting to the vehicles, they were ordered by Sam Heap to return immediately. Most of them had little or no ammunition, yet they turned and followed their leaders with no hesitation at all, back to where we were lying under our bush. Had the enemy counter-attacked, it would have been just the OC and I with a few isolated pockets of our troops scattered around. Added to which if I was to have been any use, Ferreira would have had to wake me up!

I woke up again a little later with Corporal Peter Lipman calling urgently over the radio, wanting to know what to do … he reported between thirty and forty enemy advancing towards their position against the river, north of the base. There were only three of them in his position. He was part of our group of thirty reconnaissance men deployed in sticks of three, to the north of the FAPLA base. I relayed the message to the OC. He thought for a moment, then said "Tell him he was put there as a stopper group, he must do what he was put there to do". I paused, and took a deep breath before relaying the instruction to my friend… feeling every bit as if I was sentencing him to death. It was a sentiment he seemed to share as it was with a tone of disbelief that he acknowledged. And so the three of them stood their ground and opened up on the mass of enemy troops.

He later told me that when they opened fire as ordered he had tears streaming down his face. I have always judged bravery by the extent someone is prepared to acknowledge and express fear, and it's the manner in which they control that fear that determines their courage. Pieter Lipman is a brave man. His machine-gunner, Rifleman Alberto, was soon shot in the stomach, putting him out of action. He died before we could casevac later that afternoon. Now down to just himself and Sergeant Kevin Fitzgerald they were hopelessly outnumbered, but they desperately continued to pour fire into the enemy as they advanced towards their position. They were only saved from being overrun by two of the other three-man sticks led by Sergeants Gavin Monn and Gavin Veenstra. They ran down to their aid, hitting the enemy on their flank, firing their automatic rifles along with some shoulder-fired disposable rocket launchers. The latter gave the enemy the impression there were more of them than there actually were. Those not killed soon scattered and ran for it.

Not knowing how Peter Lipman and the stopper groups were doing, I feared the worst as what was left of the FAPLA Brigade was streaming north, straight through their positions. Incredibly there were only thirty of them in scattered stopper groups sited against literally hundreds of the fleeing enemy. Of one thing I was certain and that was that they certainly had one hell of a fight on their hands. However, my fears as to their fate were to prove unfounded as they wreaked havoc amongst the enemy, with Rifleman Alberto being their

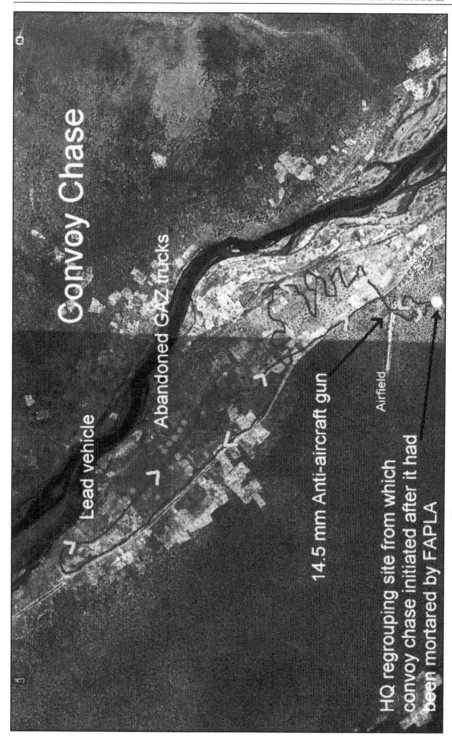

Convoy Chase

Lead vehicle

Abandoned GAZ trucks

14.5 mm Anti-aircraft gun

Airfield

HQ regrouping site from which convoy chase initiated after it had been mortared by FAPLA

The convoy chase in the late afternoon by the three Buffels.

only casualty. The fact that they were in small teams must have given them the advantage of mobility and this, combined with their aggressiveness, enabled them to account for scores of enemy dead.

I then started hearing reports that the enemy were attempting to break out to the north in a convoy, reportedly some twenty to thirty trucks with between two and three hundred troops. The convoy was avoiding the road (they had correctly guessed we had mined it) and was heading up between the road and the river. I soon heard the OCs conversation over the command net mentioning Charl Muller's name and that he might be a prisoner with the FAPLA column. He had been missing since soon after the battle began, and had last been seen bandaging his hand. We were also missing Corporal Engelbrecht and his radio operator from one of the companies. Should they be in that convoy it spelt disaster. It would have blown the lid off the clandestine nature of the operation, allowing the Angolan government to display them in Luanda for the entire world to see. Given this potential calamity, Falcon decided to throw caution to the wind, and instructed the Alouette gunship to attack the convoy. This wasn't without considerable discussion with the Air Force guys behind us. His hesitation before committing the gunship was due to the fact that it would compromise the covert aspects of our mission as UNITA did not have such gunships – only the South African Defence Force had helicopter gunships in that theatre of war.

The gunship had been sitting a few kilometres back with the rear logistics group. We soon heard the clatter of its blades and whine of the turbine as it roared over us, its single 20mm cannon sticking out the side. The pilot soon reported the convoy in sight in a calm, cool voice with the unmistakable throat rattle caused by the vibrations of a helicopter.

The engineer-gunner opened up with his cannon, firing three rounds at a time with the explosive heads hitting their targets a few seconds later. Any more than that and the chopper would be thrown out of control.

"Ba, ba, ba … … do, do, do" … … "Ba, ba, ba … … do, do, do". He hadn't fired more than a few bursts when all hell broke loose as everyone in the convoy opened up on him with automatic rifles. This was punctuated by the boom of RPG-7 anti-tank rockets, which having been fired at the chopper, would self-destruct when they failed to find their target. This went on for a considerable time and given the odds stacked against him, there came the inevitable. "We're taking rounds, we're taking rounds … … we're hit … . disengaging, disengaging!" It was the only time I heard one of those pilots on the radio sounding not so cool! The fact that our lone gunship had attacked the entire convoy single-handed was crazy anyway. He came roaring back over us, skimming over the trees at one hell-of-a speed, desperately trying to get back to the rear echelon before he fell out of the sky. I could just imagine him thumping his helicopter down in a cloud of dust and then he and the engineer-gunner running like hell, their green flying overalls flapping, in case the chopper exploded.

With that not having gone too well, the OC instructed me to request as many Buffels as possible to be sent forward. They would form a flying column that would attack the fleeing convoy. Only three Buffels arrived, one of which was our command vehicle stacked with all my Tac HQ radios. Undaunted, the OC scurried around with a spring in his step, rallying troops to volunteer for his sortie. I was making myself look as inconspicuous as possible when he spotted me loitering off to the side. "Justin! Get into your Buffel … you are coming too!" My heart sank. The OC had to be fucking crazy. Three Buffels against the entire convoy, some thirty vehicles and three hundred troops! It was with a feeling of absolute dread that I climbed up the side of the armoured vehicle. I passed my personal Machilla rucksack to one of the guys staying behind, telling him what to do with the contents should I not return. I reminded him

UNITA guide (barefoot with machete) and, possibly, Commandant
Deon Ferreira, inspecting the base the day after the attack.

about the St. Christopher I had in my pocket from my girlfriend and asked him to make sure it got back to her. I was convinced we were on a suicide mission.

There was great activity and scurrying around as we prepared ourselves, checking ammunition and weapons. From my perch up in the Buffel I noticed Corporal van Dyk emerge from the bush and called out to him. He didn't hear me in the commotion, which was a good thing. Had we made eye contact I fear the raw emotions of the day's events may well have caught up with me. As it was, I had a lump in my throat as I watched him hurry past, looking a bit dazed and with a thousand yard stare in his eyes. He had been with Sam Heap's Charlie Company which had taken a hammering to the north of the base … so much so that they had had to retreat back to our side of the airstrip. In addition, John had worked together with Captain Erasmus and Tim Patrick in the intelligence section back in the HQ … both now dead.

The Buffel's big diesels roared to life and we headed down the track towards the village. There were only about seven of us in our Buffel. The OC was sitting next to me on my right, just behind the driver so that he could shout instructions at him. The RSM sat behind us with Bruce Anders beside him. Staff-Sergeant Ron Gregory manned the Browning machine-gun mounted at the front of the Buffel. A professional soldier, he was an elderly Englishman with a wide scar on the side of his face. Some time back, an RPG anti-tank rocket had exploded in a tree next to his head. He walked and talked very deliberately as a result and was very hard of hearing. The Buffel in front of us only had about four guys in it, the machine gunner, Lieutenant Jim Ross with a 60mm mortar pipe and two others. Looking behind us at the other, I saw there were only about eight guys with Sam Heap in that vehicle. Each could have carried ten. With so few of us going up against the whole convoy, the feeling of impending doom settled even more firmly about me.

We came out of the trees and into the little 'village' of roughly five buildings that straddled the main north-south road. There were about a dozen bodies lying scattered on the ground with a few civvies wandering aimlessly around. As we roared through, I suddenly realised that the road ran up and over the end of the runway. With dread I remembered the reports coming in during the battle of one of our platoons being pinned down by a 14.5mm anti-aircraft gun that was on the end of the runway at the other side. Its huge rounds would cut through our lightly armoured Buffels from end-to-end like a hot knife through butter. Numbly I watched the Buffel ahead as it approached

Dismantling one of the dreaded 14.5mm anti-aircraft guns.

the runway, waiting for it to get cut to shreds, before the gun was then turned on us. To keep my mind off the reality, the Beatles lyrics "Picture yourself in a boat on a river, tangerine trees and marmalade skies … somebody calls you, you answer quite slowly … Lucy in the sky with diamonds … ." kept spinning over and over in my mind. Suddenly we were up on the runway and from this elevated perch I could see the smoke drifting lazily up from where the phosphorous mortar bombs had exploded earlier, off to our left and ahead. To our right, the lead Buffel had already made it into the grass, heading off between the main road on the left and the river on the right. The tail end of the convoy was about a kilometre away on the open savannah. As we came down off the end of the runway, I saw the barrel of the deadly anti-aircraft gun pointing idly up into the sky off to our left … luckily it had been abandoned.

In a flash we were over and off the end of the runway, barrelling down into the grass and low scrub, accelerating towards the convoy. The five-ton Buffel was going at speed across the open flood plain, bouncing and swaying crazily. The 7.62mm Browning in the Buffel ahead of us opened up and Jim Ross started firing a hand-held mortar pipe. How he managed to get each bomb to go towards the convoy and not straight up and back down on us I will never know. Holding the base of the mortar tube on the rubber seats of the bouncing Buffel, Jim's number two would drop the bomb down the pipe. With each detonation, the mortar pipe would bounce crazily up off the rubber seat, jumping almost above Jim's head. The pair of them were like kids, laughing each time Jim tried to control the bounce of the mortar pipe. The Buffels fanned out and all the Brownings were now firing with their characteristic stutter, tracer bullets flicking out towards the convoy … and then, of course, ours jammed! The expletives flew at poor old Ron Gregory as he struggled to clear the gun whilst being smashed around by the careening Buffel. He would manage to clear it, fire a short burst and then it would jam again. He gave up trying after a while and grabbed his rifle instead.

Having taken one look at the three Buffels charging wildly toward them, the FAPLA troops broke amongst their vehicles and ran in every direction. I also think that the mortar rounds fired by Jim Ross gave them the impression that we had a lot more firepower than we actually had. Had they stood their ground and taken us on with a few well-aimed RPG-7 rockets we would have been in serious trouble. Any semblance of co-ordination between the Buffels

A captured truck loaded with supplies. Nearly 500 weapons
and 150,000 rounds of ammunition were recovered.

soon fell apart as we each chased after a batch of the fleeing enemy.

Initially firing my rifle on semi-auto, I soon flicked to automatic fire. I had stuffed a whole case of ammunition under my seat, so with an 'unlimited' supply of rounds, I could throw caution to the wind, simply dropping my empty magazines onto the floor of the vehicle instead of having to stuff them down the front of my shirt. By this time the FAPLA troops were obviously tiring as they merely jogged along, even when my rounds found their mark and one of them would be bundled into the grass. The automatic fire thing didn't last long as I soon found that I had better control of my weapon on semi-auto, rapidly placing each shot. I can remember thinking "Now *THIS* is how you fight a war", comfortably sitting in an armoured vehicle with all the ammo I needed at my feet.

We soon ran out of targets and found ourselves alone, making heavy going of it in some bushes. Ferreira decided to make for the road and cut off the convoy by coming down at them from the front. He was in constant communication with Major Eddie Viljoen (Echo Victor) who was in a Bosbok spotter plane above us. He would tell us when to turn off the road. It was about this time that I overheard Echo Victor laughing over the VHF radio in such a

The Kavango river that runs past Savate with an Angolan
army truck that didn't make it across.

manner that it sent a chill down my spine… the FAPLA troops trying to swim across the Kavango river to escape us were getting taken by crocodiles … and he thought this was a huge joke!

We were soon accelerating gloriously up the big dirt road, revelling in the speed and the smooth ride. It suddenly dawned on me that our recce troops had mined the road leading north of the base and I reminded the OC of this. He didn't answer, just kept glancing up the road and wriggling in his seat; he was waiting for Echo Victor. "Fuck, all I need is to get blown to smithereens by one of our own mines" I thought miserably. I tightened the harness holding me into my seat and hoped for the best. Finally the call from Echo Victor came and we cut off the road into the bush, heading for the river. We came up against a seemingly impenetrable line of bushes as high as the Buffel. Echo Victor told us that what was left of the convoy was on the other side and to our right. We paused, not sure. My suggestion was to send someone on foot to check it out, lest we get taken out by an RPG as we burst through into who knew what on the other side. In addition, we couldn't be sure the line of bushes didn't conceal a bank, over which we could somersault, spilling out of the overturned Buffel in full view of the enemy … my imagination was running wild … and I was starting to lose my nerve.

The OC looked at me, then at the bushes, then back at me before deciding not to heed my advice and ordered the driver to smash through the bushes. His gamble paid off, no bank and no RPGs. Sure enough, the lead vehicle was barely eighty metres off to our right. As we charged towards it, I stood up and turned to fire over our driver's head, twisting my rifle so that the ejecting cartridges would spin up and not into the OCs face. I heard my first round hit the windscreen with a distinct crack, and the door flew open as the driver jumped out. I saw these white *tekkies* (tennis shoes) appear on the step of the cab, looking very out of place below a camouflaged uniform, before he fell out onto the ground. I fired two or three more rounds into him and he lay crumpled in a heap. I looked across at Sergeant-Major Ueckerman and saw that he had also pumped a few shots into him … he hadn't stood a chance. Almost in slow motion, with its driver's door hanging open, the truck continued forward, rolling down into a ravine and smashing into the opposite bank.

Our Buffel charged on, towards a batch of about five abandoned trucks parked one behind each other. The guys sitting behind us were firing at something when I heard a loud bang. A bit dazed, and feeling something warm and wet I looked down to see blood flowing from the back of my hand.

One of our Kwevoëls towing a captured vehicle.

"Commandant, I've been hit" I said to the OC sitting next to me. He was talking to Echo Victor over the radio and without a pause he said "Justin's hit, Justin's hit" and went right on with what he had been saying before. I felt no pain in my hand and so started checking the rest of my body, to find that I had been hit in my upper arm as well. It must have been fragments of a bullet that had disintegrated against the inside of the Buffel, spraying my arm like a shotgun. For a few years after that, I occasionally had small dark metal fragments work their way up and out of my arm. For the moment, we bandaged my arm and hand as best we could to stop the bleeding.

We circled the abandoned vehicles and then headed back as it was now getting late and we didn't have long before the sun set. We passed the body of the driver and with my emotions welling up I said bitterly, "Commandant ... I shot that fucking cunt for Tim". I had never used language like that in front of the OC and no sooner had I said it, than I realised what a stupid thing it was to say. He didn't reply but looked off into the middle distance. It had been a long day, and I suppose there was nothing more to be said.

By the time we got back to the southern part of the Savate base it was dark, and our driver got lost, driving slap-bang into a trench. As our Buffel crashed down into the other side of the trench, I saw sparks fly out of the engine. "Now we're fucked" I thought, looking anxiously around in the gloom. Ferreira used some choice expletives to describe the driver's parentage, his mother's bad choice in bringing him into the world and leaving him in no doubt as to the only thing his sister would be good for if he had one! They got on well and had a healthy respect for each other, which makes it humorous looking back. The OC was getting jumpy, we were all jumpy – we had had enough. Our front wheels were suspended in the trench, spinning in the air, whilst the back wheels were still on the ground and our tail was sticking up. While we were radioing for the other Buffel to come and pull us out, the driver put our vehicle into low ratio, four-wheel-drive and simply reversed out. Incredible!

Eventually, we made it back up to the area we had started from, and laagered for the night a little further up from where we had been mortared that afternoon. I got Bruce Anders and Lappies, the Ops Clerk, to help me dig my slit trench just off the sandy two-track road, as with my left hand in bandages, I could only use one hand. I sat with my feet in the trench, and scratching a slit in the soft sand, I dropped an Esbit (small solid fuel cooker) into it and heated some bully beef. This was the first thing I had eaten all day. My 'fire-bucket' of sweet, hot tea was refreshing and comforting. I slid thankfully into my sleeping bag with my boots still on and my rifle alongside me. Looking up through the branches I saw the familiar stars, so clear and so close I could almost touch them. I fell instantly into a deep and exhausted sleep.

I was dragged up out of my numbing sleep at dawn by one of the CSI operatives. He was battling to get comms back to his HQ in Rundu, about 400km away. I hadn't had a straight eight hours' sleep for about two weeks, and groggily checked his HF radio, battery levels, frequency, antenna connections, antenna length to frequency (exact quarter wavelength) and got him good comms with his base. He stood off to one side, watching me with a quizzical look. He had flown in the afternoon before and was wearing his clean army 'browns' and with no 'Black-is-beautiful', had a pristine, clean-shaven white face. I was sitting in the sand, crouched over his radio automatically going through the motions that now came so readily, exhausted, rumpled, unshaven, wearing filthy camouflaged battle fatigues, my face covered in three day old 'black-is-beautiful', blotched and streaked with sweat, and my left arm wrapped in dirty bandages. No doubt I didn't smell too good either, as he seemed to make a point of standing a good few metres away. Mumbling acknowledgement to his thanks, I picked up my rifle and went back to sit on the edge of my slit trench.

I made a fire-bucket of coffee and with my hands wrapped around the warmth of the drink, enjoyed the crisp morning with my elbows on my knees.

Savate village - the main street situated to the west of the
airfield and straddling the main north-south road.

Our recce troops inspecting the vehicles in the convoy that was stopped heading north.

Cmdt Oelschig, Chief Staff Intelligence and Cmdt Deon Ferreira,
Officer Commanding, 32 Battalion. (Courtesy of Piet Nortje)

Everything looked fresh in the cool air, and it was good to be alive. The previous day's events hung heavily in the back of my mind. It was the start of a long process of sifting through conflicting emotions in order to come to terms with it all. We were sent back up to the convoy we had hit north of the base, spending the morning searching through the abandoned vehicles and blowing them up when we were done. There was a huge amount of kit on the back of the trucks and I scored an AK-47 bayonet off a pile on one of them, and two sets of Russian artillery binoculars from behind the seats of another. There must have been about forty sets there; a huge pity to see them go up in flames. We were searching around the head of the convoy when one of the guys scouting out ahead came up short with a grimace on his face. He had found the body of the driver the RSM and I had shot to pieces. For years after that I was to have a recurring nightmare … one where I would be walking through the grass and would come across the bleached bones of the driver sticking through what was left of his tattered uniform.

We were at the tail end of the convoy when a shout went up. A FAPLA soldier was coming out of the reed bed next to the river, AK-47 in hand. From

Heading home on a captured vehicle.

Loading 'Stalin Organ' or 'Monakashita' rockets onto one of our Kwevoëls.

up in the Buffel, my R1 rifle came effortlessly into my shoulder. As I centred my sights on his chest, one of the intelligence guys shouted "Don't shoot, don't shoot, we need him as a prisoner". Leaving nothing to chance, I kept my sights on him saying quietly to myself "run you motherfucker... run", willing him to try and escape so that I could drop him. What the *hell* had come over me?!

They disarmed him, pushing him up into the Buffel. He had a real attitude that earned him a good few '*klaps*' around the head to remind him who was who. We took him back to the rear echelon area from where he was choppered out in one of the big Pumas, together with a handful of other prisoners, back to Rundu.

As it turned out, Charl Muller hadn't been on the convoy as they had found his body late the previous afternoon. He had been shot at close range in the back of his head before being dumped into the bottom of a trench. However, Corporal Engelbrecht and his radio operator were still missing.

We went back down to the village to meet up with the OC. It was late in the morning now and we were parked just south of the village. The RSM had commandeered a really cool, open Toyota Land Cruiser that was parked nearby. He was waxing lyrical about how he was going to cruise around back in Rundu in his piece of war booty. I could just picture it, broad chest puffed out, big red handle-bar moustache ruffling in the wind with his camouflaged 32 Battalion beret at a rakish angle, when with an ear splitting 'Cabooom', the bonnet of his treasured Land Cruiser went sailing up into the air. "*Wat die fok?*" ("What the fuck?") he shouted, his mouth falling open and speechless for once. Rick Lobb, from the recce teams, had fired an RPG-7 anti-tank rocket into the engine block to see what effect it would have!

The OC arrived soon after with Echo Victor and a CSI operative. While we were catching up relating the day's events, the CSI guy moved off to take a photo of us (see next page). They were the only ones allowed cameras on such sensitive operations. I was resting my injured hand up on the spare wheel of the Buffel as it was bothering me and especially hurt when it was hanging free. My back is to the vehicle in the photo. I'm talking to Rick Lobb and someone else who has his back to the camera. Major Eddie Viljoen (Echo Victor) is on the left with Commandant Ferreira second from the left. Two whip antennas are visible from the radio sets I had built into the command Buffel. Ron Gregory had taken his errant Browning machine-gun off as can be seen by the empty mount on the top of the Buffel. True to the toughness of these vehicles, no damage is visible on the front of the vehicle from dropping into the trench the

Left to right: Cmdt Deon Ferreira, Maj Schutte, Sgt-Maj Ueckerman, Capt
Sam Heap (bandaged face), Cmdt Oelschig CSI, Capt Jim Ross.

Left to right: Major Eddie Viljoen, Cmdt Deon Ferreira, Cpl Rick Lobb, unknown
(back to camera), 2Lt Justin Taylor, with bandaged hand up on the spare wheel.

UNITA guide working with the CSI, standing with AK-47 in the town.

night before. This photo was kept along with others in a photo album in the intelligence room back at the HQ at Rundu. Of the other photos, one was of the mobile tank-tracked pontoon bridges that we had discovered in the base.

The OC and I stood off to one side of the group for a while, quietly discussing some operational issues and the previous day's events. I remember him characteristically shifting the pistol on his belt and pursing his lips as he talked about the difficulty he had had in controlling the battle once it had begun. In fact, he said, he had to accept early in the battle that he was unable to control it and had to place his trust in his company and platoon commanders, commenting that they had more information at hand anyway to evaluate the situation and make the right decisions. His conclusion was once the battle begins, trust the judgment of the officers and NCOs you have in place, leave it to these leaders on the ground and let the operation run its course. He learned at Savate that it is impossible to micro-manage battle. Ferreira was one of the most amazing leaders I have been fortunate to work with. He was an energetic, enigmatic, compassionate and scholarly officer who inspired those around him and led by example. He had a knack for effective strategic appreciation and as a result his planning was strategically inspired. He used the orders process in a clear and concise way to communicate his combat objectives, to promote and

CSI operative posing in front of a South African Buffel.

CSI operative with Commandant Oelschig in front of a Soviet-supplied Angolan Army truck.

enthuse. His success at the Battle of the Lomba River in 1987/88, when he wiped out a FAPLA Brigade through brilliant tactical soldiering, came as no surprise, nor did the fact that he later rose to the rank of Major General and to become Chief of Joint Operations for the South African Defence Force.

At one point a group of about twenty civvies appeared out of the reeds along the river. They had obviously taken refuge there during the battle. They began moving back towards the village, taking a path that would bring them past where we were standing next to the vehicles. One of the CSI guys got very agitated at this prospect and began firing over their heads, waving them away excitedly by flapping his arms above his head. He didn't want them to get too close and to see that through the 'black-is-beautiful', we were white and not black UNITA soldiers. I suppose he had a point, but it seemed a bit melodramatic at the time.

We moved up to the area where we had been mortared the day before and began assembling to move south, back across the border to Omauni. Sometime that afternoon there was a huge commotion just the other side of the airfield ... explosions and the sound of Monakashitas whooshing off in all directions. On enquiring over the radio as to what was going on, we were told by Willem Ratte's guys that they were blowing up the ammunition they couldn't carry. Willem later told me that on Staff Sergeant Ron Gregory's suggestion, rather than blow up the Monakashitas, they should pile them into the trenches and light a fire above them. Ron's thinking was that the fire would set off the explosive warheads and the ordnance would blow up. But what actually happened was that the fire ignited the rocket propellant, sending them whizzing off in all directions to explode amongst the entire Battalion, who were taking cover wherever they could. Willem to this day still doesn't know how anyone was not hurt or killed in the process!

Whilst waiting for the convoy to form up, from my perch up on top of the Buffel, I saw Willem for the first time since seeing him off at Omauni before the attack. He was loping up alongside the row of vehicles with his characteristically easy gait, looking very relaxed and generally pleased with himself. It was good to see him again, and when I asked him about his recce of the base, he showed me where he and Trooper Joao had walked in the dead of night to check out the layout of the base. They had been barely five metres from the trench line at one point and had been challenged by a FAPLA sentry. Joao had responded in his fluent, native Angolan Portuguese and the sentry had let them go on their way. The sheer nerve of it made my blood run cold!

Loading captured supplies from a Soviet-supplied Angolan
Army vehicle onto a South African Kwevoël.

A Soviet Ifa truck.

While we were waiting for all the vehicles to form up, a civilian twin-engine aircraft appeared high overhead. Stories started flying around of the last time this had happened on one of the previous ops, Angolan air force MiG fighters had arrived soon after to bomb and strafe the Battalion's positions. Although I think our cover had run a bit thin once we had used the gunship the day before, we were still trying to make out we were UNITA. So no air cover from our air force would have been forthcoming had we been attacked by MiGs. From the miserable faces around me I could see I wasn't the only one glancing anxiously to the north, the direction in which the civvy aircraft had departed. To my relief, the convoy started moving slowly forward and we began the long trek back.

I can't remember if we drove through the night or if we stopped soon after dark. However, it seemed we did stop to refuel and take stock of the situation

The architects of victory and the commanders at the Battle of Savate - Cmdt Oelschig, Chief Staff Intelligence (left) and Cmdt Deon Ferreira, Officer Commanding, 32 Battalion. Looking tired after the battle, Ferreira still has 'black-is-beautiful' on his face and carries his coveted AKM, the folding stock AK-47 assault rifle. Photos taken by a CSI operative the day after the Battle of Savate. (Courtesy of Piet Nortje)

This and next three pages: 45 Soviet-supplied Angolan Army vehicles were destroyed and 10 brought back by 32 Bn. These were in addition to those that escaped to the north.

at about mid-morning the next day. One of the doctors examined my arm and hand and decided that I needed to get back to the hospital in Rundu. About the same time, the order came in over the big HF radios in the command Buffel that the Battalion had to return to Savate. Corporal Engelbrecht and his radio operator were still missing. The order was that we were not to leave Angola until they had been found. Boy … was I relieved I wasn't going with them! I had visions of the Battalion being wiped out by hordes of avenging FAPLA troops swarming down from the north. I could see the OC wasn't happy with me not being there and I could see him pondering whether to overrule the doc. I think he was a bit suspicious that I may have set the doc up to send me home!

The convoy disappeared back up the track towards Savate and I waited with the rear echelon group for a Puma to arrive later that afternoon, on its way back from a CSI mission deep into Angola, which was probably a liaison meeting with UNITA. At around midday, the report came through that they had found the bodies of Corporal Engelbrecht and his radioman. They had gone to ground early in the battle having been wounded and had sought to wait the action out. A large group of FAPLA had then run into them as they headed off into the bush after the Three-Two troops had overrun their trenches.

TOP SECRET/UITERS GEHEIM   DD1991
OPERATIONS WAR DIARY/OORLOGSDAGBOEK OPERASIES
OF/VAN   BAND/VOLUME..............
MAAND/MONTH..............
PLEK   TYDPERK VAN   TOT
PLACE....................................PERIOD FROM...................TO ....

Reeks no. Serial no.	Datum en tyd Date and time	Opsomming van voorvalle en informasie Summary of events and information	Verwysing Reference
4	23/1800/6	Silup no 3 ... Period 24/1700/6 — 23/1700/6 May 80 ...	Ops/2/2/Maye
5	23/1920/6	Small Resistance informed us this side that their present log stat is BXC and that they are moving out to the base tonight.	Informal.
2 Lt G Taylor (Sig off) ... troop who sustained shrapnel wounds during the attack on Savate was flown in to this base today for medical attention 2Lt Taylor had shrapnel wounds through the left hand. He returned to Rundu today by air. Lt Hedy got shrapnel in the chin but remained with convoy.			Informal.

OPS/1/32 BN   TOP SECRET/UITERS GEHEIM

War Diary entry from Omauni referring to when 2Lt Taylor was casevac'd out of Angola in a Puma helicopter after being wounded two days before, at Savate. (Courtesy of Piet Nortje)

Scores of dead bodies had been found scattered in front of the position as the two men had valiantly fought to the end. When I received the big portable HF radio back at the HQ a few weeks later, it had been literally shot to pieces. A Puma was despatched from Omauni to fetch Corporal Engelbrecht's body, while that of the troop for some reason was to stay with the convoy. I was to get a ride on this Puma and not wait for the CSI chopper.

It landed in a grass clearing in front of us and doubled over, I ran out to it. I sat on the floor of the chopper with my back to the side. Engelbrecht was a big red-headed guy who couldn't fit into the body bag. They had cut two holes for his feet to stick out. The minute the chopper lifted off and they slid the big side door shut, a nauseating odour emitted through the holes cut into the bag and wafted across the cabin … his body had been lying out in the heat of the bush for two days. An infantry Major who was a 'camper', and who had been sent up from his cattle farm in the Natal Midlands for border experience was in the chopper as well. A logistics co-ordinator, he was a well meaning guy at heart, who had been telling us only a few weeks before how lucky we were to be experiencing such an adventure as the Border War. By now I was feeling decidedly sorry for myself … my arm had a dull throbbing pain and Corporal Engelbrecht lay in his body bag next to me, with the odour strong in my nostrils.

When our eyes met across the chopper, the Major knew that I was thinking about our last conversation. He could see the words "*Ja*, fat adventure this is" stencilled in my eyes. He reached across and grasped my shoulder in a gesture of support, and looked at me with compassion and understanding. Not that there was much to say, but if there had been, it would have been impossible to hear even when shouted over the roar of the blades and twin turbines driving the big Puma. I sat in my own cocoon of thoughts, relieved to be skimming at speed just above the treetops back to our side of the border. It was great to get back to Omauni and it was a real treat to get some freshly cooked food in the mess.

I was to travel the remainder of the flight in a Kudu. I walked out to the light aircraft once they had sorted whatever admin had to be done and to my dismay saw Corporal Engelbrechts' body in there. The forty-minute Puma ride was bad enough, but another hour's flying in the close confines of the Kudu was going to be another story. Also on board was an Intelligence guy with a SWAPO prisoner from the west somewhere. The devious Intelligence Officer spent the whole flight asking him confusing, roundabout questions trying to get him to compromise himself and part with sensitive information. I closed my mind to the interrogation and the odour from the body bag, and lost myself in thoughts of civvy-street … home … the beach … surfing on a crystal blue sea at sunrise. We arrived back at the big army base in Rundu at last light.

To my embarrassment, I was met by an ambulance with its light flashing. I told them in no uncertain terms that I could walk to the hospital, but they bundled me into the back before I could argue. I hoped none of my mates would see me. At the hospital I was told to have a good shower, given some hospital pyjamas and put into a ward full of 32 Battalion guys. The black troop next to me was badly burned, probably by a phosphorous grenade similar to that which killed Tim Patrick. He was covered almost completely with sticky yellow gauze patches and lay very still the whole night. We all had drips hooked up to our arms. When I woke up in the morning, I saw the bed next to me was empty. The troop had died in the night. It was only by mid-morning that they got to clean the bed, which was covered in foul, sticky yellow swabs.

Sometime in the afternoon, the medic came to inject the next course of drugs into my drip which flowed into my arm. As the penicillin he injected hit my bloodstream, my mind remained crystal clear while I lost complete control of my arms and legs, which began to flap around alarmingly. The medic stood there looking at me with his mouth open and I had to tell him several times to fetch the doctors. Two of them came running in and stood at my bedside, not knowing quite what to do. After a few minutes the spasms subsided and my body quietened, and I suddenly broke down, sobbing unashamedly with tears streaming down my face. The emotions I was battling with had finally come to the fore, aided by fatigue and the drugs they had pumped into me. One of the doctors was a dentist and he had done an excellent filling a few weeks before, which has lasted to this day some thirty years on. I managed to crack a smile when he asked if at least my dental filling was ok?!

We had scarcely more than begun to know what living meant, but we all knew about dying and for many, the experience was to leave upon some minds the deepest of scars.

Sholto Douglas, RFC in Denis Winter's *The First of the Few* (WWI)

32 Battalion colours: Honesty Loyalty Justice

Eerlikheid Lojaliteit Regverdigheid: Honestidade Lealidade Justica

The background of the unit colour is rifle green with the fringe in black and gold, the colours of the South African Infantry Corps. The unit badge is a silver buffalo head with two crossed arrows with the scroll underlining the buffalo head. Large quantities of buffalo are found in the vicinity of 32 Battalion's training base, Buffalo. The presence of this gracious, fearless, proud animal led to the unit adopting this as the official unit badge. Seeing that the unit originated during the Angolan war of 1975, the motto *Proelio Procusi,* which means 'Forged in Battle', is literally applicable. (32 Battalion colours photo courtesy of Piet Nortje.)

1

Basic training. Kit inspection, with the ever-shouting Corporal on left.

Basic training. *Jippoing* ... when the Corporal is away the Signaller will play.

End of basic training - Signalman Taylor trying to look cool with his 'chick'!

Officers' course - CO A. Sender in the ubiquitous army 'Garry', or Land Rover.

32 Battalion Ops Room, Rundu, Christmas Eve 1979. Left to right: 2Lt Justin Taylor, Candidate Officer (later 2Lt) Tim Patrick, Cpl John van Dyk (seated), Signalman 'Gonzales'. Note the hat rack as the Christmas tree, decorated with an R1 assault rifle, 9mm Star pistol, dog tags, bush hat, 32 beret, can of beans and a bible.

The ubiquitous 'Flossie' arriving in the Operational Area, a photo taken by author in 1983 from Fort Rev, the 5 Recce base at Ondangwe

Impala landing with empty bomb racks. Note the Bofors anti-aircraft gun on the tower in the background), Oshakati Air Force Base. Both photos on this page taken by author in 1983 from Fort Rev, the 5 Recce base.

Two heavily-laden Impala ground strike jets getting airborne in a southerly direction before turning north to Angola.

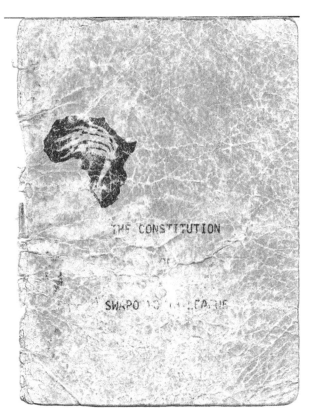

Captured documents from Operation Butterfly. These were some
of the documents captured with Commander Hindongo east of
Chana Umbi and during other contacts in that operation.

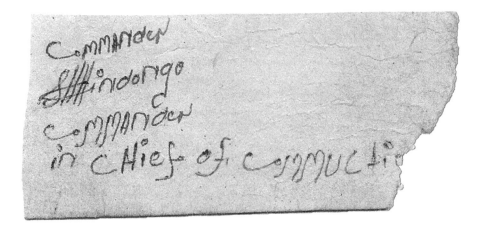

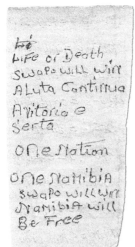

Captured documents from Operation Butterfly. The perforation in the photo was caused by the shrapnel from the 20mm cannon in the helicopter gunship that killed the guerrilla fighter. His bloodstained ID photo is above.

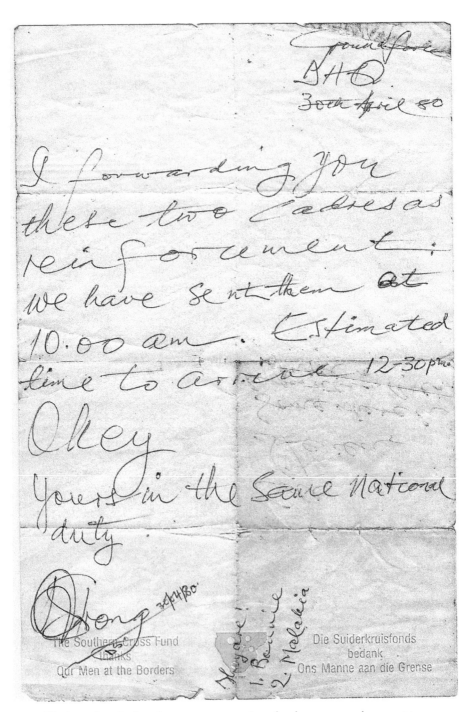

GroundForce
BHQ
30th April 80

I forwarding you these two cadres as reinforcement. We have sent them at 10.00 am. Estimated time to arrive 12.30 pm.

Okey

Yours in the Same National duty.

Strong 30/4/80

The Southern Cross Fund thanks Our Men at the Borders

1. Bonnie
2. Malakia

Die Suiderkruisfonds bedank Ons Manne aan die Grense

The irony here is that the message was written by the enemy on letter writing stationery provided to the South African soldiers by the Southern Cross Fund (an organisation founded to support the morale of the SA troops)!

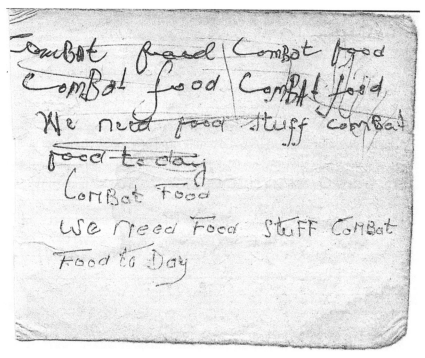

A guerrilla fighter's poignant notes to his 'lady'.

His scribbled logistics messages.

Signalling course instructors, all Savate vets. Left to right, rear: Sgt Gav Veenstra, 2Lt Justin Taylor, Cpl John van Dyk, seated: Sgt 'Daisy' Loubscher, Sgt Tabo Maree. All carry Soviet AK-47 assault rifles with chest webbing containing spare magazines. 2Lt Justin Taylor has the handset for the VHF radio used for inter-platoon and ground-to-air communication on the left of his chest webbing for ease of use. This was standard practice amongst the platoons.

Signalling course. The Tac HQ with a Buffel armoured troop carrier parked alongside.

Signalling course. Sgt 'Daisy' Loubscher instructing on the Soviet RPD machine gun.

Signalling course. 2Lt Justin Taylor firing his Soviet AK-47 assault
rifle. Note the VHF (A72) ground-to-air radio used for command and
control purposes strapped to his waist on the 'first-line webbing'.

Signalling course. One of the troops firing the Soviet RPK (essentially a heavy-
barrelled AK-47) with Sgt Gavin Veenstra looking on as the instructor.

Signalling course. Sgt Gavin Veenstra instructing on the 1960s-vintage
Heckler & Koch HK21 machine gun (Germany). With a cog that mechanically
drew the belt into the chamber, it had an incredibly high rate of fire.

Signalling course. Weapon assembly competition. The winning team, with the coveted
prize of a jug of warm orange juice - Sgt Veenstra, Corporal Prior, Corporal Bodley
(squatting), Signalman Knoetze, Signalman Base, Signalman Nel, 2Lt MacMillan.

Signalling course. 2Lt MacMillan enjoying a well-earned cup of
tea while posing with his standard issue R1 assault rifle.

Signalling course. Getting ready for the night security patrol. Corporal
Peter Price checks his rifle's magazine, centre right.

Signalling course - Corporal Shaun Prior mans the 60mm commando mortar pipe. He is about to drop a mortar bomb into the tube, which detonated a cartridge at the base of the bomb, shooting it out of the tube. On impacting the ground, the high explosive bomb would explode.

32 Battalion Signals course, final selection - Signallers boarding the Buffels.

32 Battalion Signals course, final selection. Signallers in a
Buffel, blindfolded for the ride to the drop-off points.

32 Battalion Signals course, final selection. 2Lt Justin Taylor
tracking the progress of the teams overnight.

The candidates that passed the 32 Battalion Signals course. They were awarded their berets by Commandant Ferreira at the battalion HQ in Rundu. Standing left to right: Signalman (Smn) C. Kempkin-Smith, Smn C. Kirshov, Smn R. Mann, Cpl P. Price, Cpl J. Bodley, Smn C. Wessels, Smn M. Pitschlitz, Smn S. Base, Smn C. deWet, Smn T. Nel, Smn M. Knoetze. Seated left to right: 2Lt Justin Taylor (Signals Officer), Major Eddie Viljoen (2IC), Commandant Deon Ferreira (OC), Sergeant-Major Ueckerman (RSM).

Those selected as the Signals team to be used on external, cross-border operations. Left to right, standing - Signalman (Smn) C. Kempkin-Smith, Smn S. Base, Smn C. Kirshov; seated – 2d Lt Justin Taylor (Signals Officer), Cpl J. Bodley (Signals Troop NCO).

Savate Day Memorial Service, Zeerust, 2008.
The Tree of Remembrance that was initially at Buffalo Base in the Caprivi was
kept at 2 SA Infantry Base in Zeerust after 32 Battalion was disbanded. I flew out
for the memorial service, my beret poignantly placed on the instrument panel.

Savate Day Memorial Service, Savate, 21 May 2012 – thirty-two years to the day that the battle began. Veterans of the battle at the memorial. Left to right: Peter Lipman, Nico Groenewald, Leon Grobler, Justin Taylor, Rick Lobb, Mike Kylie.

Savate Day Memorial Service, Savate, 21 May 2012 – thirty-two years to the day that the battle began. Saluting the memorial thirty-two years later to the day, to the hour, that the battle began, 21 May, 9am Angolan time.

Savate Day Memorial Service, Savate, 21 May 2012 – thirty-two years to the day that the battle began. Former enemies, Justin Taylor and an Angolan official.

Savate, 21 May 2012 – thirty-two years to the day that the battle began. The Soviet pontoon bridge the day after the battle, and below, thirty-two years later, Justin Taylor standing on the same spot.

Savate, 21 May 2012 – thirty-two years to the day that the battle began. A Russian BRDM armoured troop carrier the day after the battle, and below, thirty-two years later, Justin Taylor standing next to what could well be the same BRDM now lying on its back.

Savate, 21 May 2012: thirty-two years to the day that the battle began.
Part of the trench system the day after the battle, and below, thirty-two years
later, Justin Taylor standing in the trenches assaulted by Alpha Company, closely
followed by the HQ element, only to find enemy still in the trenches.

Savate, 21 May 2012 – thirty-two years to the day that the battle began. Unexploded ordnance still lying on the battlefield. Pedro, the Angolan battlefield guide, holds a Soviet 82mm mortar bomb. His services were essential as the area was still heavily mined.

10

Home

The next day was a Sunday and some mates told me there was a Flossie filled with cargo returning to Pretoria that afternoon. Tim Patrick's funeral was to be later in the week down in Natal and they could organise a jump seat for me if I could get out of hospital. I told them to go ahead and organise the seat as I would discharge myself then and there. I got up and was pulling the drip out of my arm when the medic came in and had a coronary! He told me I was supposed to stay till Wednesday and that I was not allowed to leave and threatened to call the doctor. The drip was out by then and I told him he may as well call the doctor as I had made my decision. After all, this was the medic who had nearly killed me the day before, so fuck him. He called the doctor but by the time he arrived I was already in my army browns with my boots on. When I explained that I had an opportunity to catch a lift on the Flossie that afternoon, to get back to my mate's funeral, there was not much he could say. It wasn't as if I was dying in his hospital anyway, it was just a small shrapnel wound. Whilst he wasn't too happy, he sorted me a bag of pills and gave me the instructions that went with them.

My girlfriend was doing her nursing training at Greys Hospital in Pietermaritzburg at the time. She spotted me coming down the street, arm in a sling and dressed in my standard SA Army 'browns', my Three-Two boots and camouflaged beret – I thought I looked quite cool. In a scene straight out of a movie, she came running out in her white nursing uniform and squeaky brown shoes to throw her arms around me. The funeral was really awkward, as I couldn't tell Tim Patrick's family what happened, having to stick to the story that was in the newspapers. We had supposedly run into a massive ambush in South West Africa, resulting in the deaths of the white 32 Battalion guys. Our black KIA didn't crack a mention as they were stateless, being neither South African nor Angolan citizens. Even *Time* magazine were duped, they reported the Battle of Savate as a significant UNITA victory.

The initial intrigue around the clandestine nature of the war we were fighting began to wear very thin. Dealing with the emotional issues while not being able to talk about them, turned out to be increasingly difficult. My university friends were living their student life … beer, cars and girls. While I could certainly see the attractions, I couldn't relate to it. My worldly possessions were a rifle, my Machilla rucksack and what fitted in a *balsak* (kit bag). I needed money only to buy chocolate and a few beers when in base. Everything I did revolved around the singular issues of life and death and there were no grey areas in between. It was a very simple existence. I just couldn't see the relevance of what they found important.

I had been given two weeks R & R and returned to the unit after only a week. I had been back at the HQ in Rundu for only a few weeks when it was tactfully suggested (in a way that I knew I didn't have an option) that I should take my full annual fourteen days leave. I skipped my Varsity mates this time and went straight back to the family farm in Zululand. It was really awesome spending time at home with all that was familiar. When my mother asked me about the wound in my arm, she wanted to know if I had had to fire my machine-gun during the battle. "Something like that" I replied with a wry smile. My elder brother told me about the incident when a couple of days after Savate (about which he had no idea), the local *Dominee* (Afrikaans priest) had excitedly rushed onto the golf course to officially inform him that I had been wounded. Given that it wasn't a serious injury, it was certainly a bit melodramatic – but what did he know?! I often took the farm's Land Rover, a shotgun and the dogs and spent a lot of time sitting on the sand banks of the Umfolozi River. With the dogs sitting comfortingly around me, I stared blankly into the muddy water as it slid idly past.

Savate … I tried to filter the emotions that swirled through my mind, my thoughts locked in, firmly internalized as I was unable to discuss any of it with anyone. This was possibly the hardest part of clandestine operations. It was almost impossible to discuss the personal aspects without the detail of where and why. And finding someone who would be able to relate to it all to help you come to terms with it was unlikely. The excitement, the pride, the unquestionable camaraderie, the exhaustion, the fear, the bravery and tenacity, the exhilaration, the anguish, the guilt, the grief, the emptiness. The one emotion that slowly came to the fore was the guilt … and surprisingly this was not about the men I had killed. The killing had been easy, too easy. Maybe that was the training, and it was, after all, a fair fight (in fact the odds had been stacked heavily against us). Somehow my ambivalence with this aspect doesn't worry me. It is an emptiness which I have come to terms with over the years.

Strangely the guilt I carried is that I survived. My close friends Tim Patrick

ID photo taken whilst on leave ... "I thought I was smiling
for the camera ... Savate had left its mark."

and Heinz Muller didn't. Tim had a preoccupied, detached look in his eye the last time I saw him, but there again, it was the first time he was going into combat. Heinz knew he was not going to make it ... "Justin, *jy moet lekker wees*" haunted me. The bullet that missed my neck by inches, the one that fragmented before hitting my arm, Captain Erasmus shot dead a couple of metres from me ... what determines the throw of the dice? Who knows?! It took me years to find a balance ... life is a gift, whether you live for one day or a hundred years ... cherish every day you are able to look up and see the deep blue sky, the beautiful green grass and the flitting bird flashing from branch to branch ... so full of life and enthusiasm. Embrace it, cherish it, revel in it – above all, find the goodness and the happiness. That's what those who have passed on would want for us. Grief is a healthy emotion that you can't and shouldn't deny, and to dwell on it too long is simply self-pity. Life for them is over. We owe it to them to get on with what is left of ours. Death is unavoidable. When it's time ... its time. Face it, accept it.

Again, I lasted only a week as I struggled to even relate to my own close and very dear family. I am not sure they understood when I tried to explain that I needed to be back on the border and to face what I had to do there until I had completed my National Service. With that obligation behind me, I felt I could then come back and readjust to civvy life … I couldn't be in between … it needed to be one thing at a time.

So I was back in Rundu early again. This time they didn't send me home but left me to my own devices. It was good to be back and to settle into the routine with which I had become so familiar. But things in the HQ were now very different. Of five Battalion HQ officers who had gone into the battle, only two of us had survived, Commandant Ferreira and myself. Captain Erasmus, Charl Muller and Tim Patrick didn't make it. I never even got to write the signals de-brief for Savate as I had for every other Op we'd undertaken. Every time I tried, I just stared blankly at the sheet of paper in front of me. The photo taken for ID purposes while I was on leave seems to say a lot; I thought I was smiling at the time. Savate had left its mark.

We had attacked against overwhelming odds, 350 against what turned out to be possibly as many as 1,400 of the enemy. Fifteen dead and nearly sixty wounded on our side, with radio intercepts later confirming that FAPLA had suffered some 558 killed, wounded or missing. Even given 32 Battalion's' personnel losses, militarily it was a significant success. Ferreira's calculated risk of attacking when he knew that we were outnumbered and when we had lost the element of surprise by not attacking at dawn, paid off, as had his decision not to change the battle plan.

Alpha Company up ahead of us in the HQ had taken the brunt of the fight. They had the widest area to cover and took the most casualties, losing their Company Commander and Intelligence Officer early in the fight. The company was led by the platoon commanders and section leaders, who not knowing their company commander was already dead, were puzzled as to why they couldn't raise him on the radio. They nonetheless fought their way through to their objectives on the other side of the base, arriving on the far side of the little village battered, bewildered and almost out of ammunition. Pinned down and having left a number of their own dead and wounded behind them, they began to be rightly concerned that these would fall prey to the enemy. Being almost out of ammunition, they were highly vulnerable to counter-attack. Fortunately, Foxtrot Company came to the rescue.

Foxtrot, attacking off to our right under the command of Lt Jim Ross, also came under withering fire, with their descriptions of trees exploding above their heads and leaves falling like snow around them. Despite also taking considerable casualties, they emerged on the other side of the base as an organised and coherent fighting unit. And they certainly appeared to save the day as Jim Ross regrouped his company and came back across to help out the tattered remnants of Alpha Company. His steadfast leadership was welcomed by the Alpha Company platoon commanders and it delivered solid command and control to them in the absence of their own company commander, who they now knew was missing, though they were unaware had been killed.

Willem Ratte had played a key role from his OP (Observation Post) on the eastern banks of the river, directing accurate mortar fire on critical areas needing support and most notably silencing the 14.5mm anti-aircraft gun. The lone air force spotter plane had also been decisive, as this 'eye-in-the-sky' with Echo Victor (Major Eddie Viljoen) had given us continuous and critical information regarding enemy movements, making it easier for Ferreira to make his tactical decisions. It had also been able to relay messages when there were communication problems with the smaller VHF sets due to terrain or the instance of commanders being killed.

The desperate nature of the battle illustrated the knife-edge on which the outcome of the assault had teetered, particularly as the full extent of by how much we were outnumbered became apparent. By mid-afternoon we had fired off all our 81mm mortar rounds and had nothing in reserve in case of a counter-attack. And to their superior numbers the enemy had added a show of discipline and considerable courage. Being regular Angolan army troops, they had laid down a blistering, vicious and disciplined field of fire from a well-prepared trench system. In addition, they had chosen to fight and where possible, retreat ... but not to surrender.

With the two commanders effectively eyeball to eyeball, it was then that Ferreira's superior tactical appreciation began to tell. He knew we had taken the southern part of the base, and made the right decision to support Sam Heap's request to withdraw his company from the northern side of the airfield and regroup with the other two companies on the south. This left the enemy in a precarious position, knowing that there was a large force in control of the commanding high ground to the south of the airfield. It was at this point that they would appear to have lost their nerve. They attempted to break out to the north after mortaring us mid-afternoon, straight into the reconnaissance teams deployed as stopper groups, albeit only thirty men in groups of three. The tenacity with which the vastly outnumbered reconnaissance guys had taken on the retreating enemy had left them confused as to where the attack was coming from, and fostered the illusion that they were up against considerably more men than was the case. Deploying the lone gunship in a desperate attempt at halting the convoy seriously jeopardised the clandestine nature of the whole operation. However, it was a risk worth taking as Ferreira believed our missing men were being held captive, with the intention of FAPLA getting them back to Luanda to display to the world. The damage the single 20mm cannon inflicted on the convoy ensured there was no hope of an organized retreat.

Then Ferreira initiated the convoy chase ... with the same élan as Wellington had shown at the Battle of Waterloo when he let loose his cavalry on Napoleon. However, that's where the similarity ends as we were a far more ragged, tatty looking bunch than those dashing cavalry types! Again, completely outnumbered and against the odds ... three Buffels with about fifteen of us against reports of thirty vehicles and some 300 enemy troops. We hit the tail end of what was left of the convoy and they finally disintegrated, splintered and ran. Ferreira's combat appreciation, his assessment of risk and his timing was uncanny. We had gone up against overwhelming odds and won the day. What strikes me looking back was the tenacity and confidence of the troops, officers and NCOs. It was the unflinching, steady, methodical nature of the men that carried the day for us, testimony to the Battalion's leadership and the outstanding quality of the troops.

With the Battle of Savate, the irony remains that Three-Two had not been given the go-ahead by Pretoria for the attack. The signal that came through to Commandant Ferreira and Commandant Oelschig was very ambiguous in its directive. The brass back in Pretoria maintained that they had given the go-ahead for the reconnaissance of the base only, yet the wording was such that Ferreira and Oelschig took it as formal approval for a full-scale attack. Be that as it may, in the bigger scheme of things Savate was the turning point for UNITA's war in the region. It gave them the confidence that South Africa was indeed behind their initiative to dominate the entire south-eastern part of Angola. The domino effect was that other FAPLA towns in the region soon fell to UNITA, and FAPLA withdrew from the region. Strategically and at the time, this was a significant and notable success.

11

Convoy commander

In my first operation after Savate I got to be convoy commander on an operation with Willem Ratte and his Recce Group to the north-west of the Omauni base.

I had to bring extra Buffels out from Rundu to Omauni and had lined the convoy up in the middle of the big Rundu army base with myself positioned in the middle. Never having been a convoy commander before, I thought this was the logical spot to place myself in – besides, I was pretty sure that this is where Field Marshal Rommel would have placed himself. Having completed a radio check with both the lead and the tail-end vehicle, and with Rommel firmly in mind, I barked the command to advance. As the convoy began to rumble out of the base, a shout went up from the rear. Looking back I saw 'Jan Ops' had exploded out of the Battalion HQ command bunker and was running wildly towards me shouting … *"Leuitnant wag … Leuitnant WAG!"* ("Lieutenant wait … Lieutenant WAIT!") Thinking a great calamity was about to befall us, I barked into the radio, "Convoy … HALT!" (… that Rommel thing again). The entire convoy ground to a halt and with all the vehicle engines idling away, dozens of eyes watched me expectantly.

I looked down from my Buffel at Ops Jan as he drew up alongside me, wide-eyed and out of breath. Raising his voice above the rumble of the big diesels he said, "Lieutenant … your girlfriend phoned to say … (pant, pant) … that your elder brother … (pant, pant) … has just had a baby daughter", and then put his hands on his knees to get his breath back. Ops Jan used to take all the phone calls coming into the HQ. I never knew what my girlfriend used to say to him when she phoned, but she certainly struck the fear of God into him! He always came running to find me wherever I was and interrupt whatever I was doing, at any time of day or night. Looking at the guys in the Buffel with me I could see wry smiles, smirking at my embarrassment … quietly discarding the Rommel act, I cleared my throat and instructed the convoy to advance again.

Having headed west and got the convoy safely from Rundu to Omauni, we then deployed to the north-west of Omauni. Willem Ratte and a small team went in on foot to recce a suspected gook base. Once it was identified, Willem was to call us in to assault the enemy camp. The cool thing was that travelling in the Buffel meant I didn't have to carry everything in my Machilla backpack, so I had every luxury I could lay my hands on. As it was July and freezing cold at night, I had two sleeping bags, a sack full of cool drinks, fistfuls of chocolate and another sack full of tinned fruit I had raided from the chefs back at base. I called these 'Morale Boosters' and I had great fun handing them out at any opportunity to anyone passing my Buffel.

The operation as a whole was good fun as we tried to use some ex mounted-infantry horses the recce guys had found roaming in the bush. These were to resupply Willem and his recce teams – no giving the game away by sending in the noisy Puma helicopters! Some innovative logistics guy organised high protein hay from a mounted infantry unit off to our west somewhere. Overcharged with their energy boost from the hay, the horses took off like rockets as each guy hit the saddle, disappearing at full gallop into the bush. All but one rider was thrown off. One guy fell off when the horse did a right angle turn to miss a bush; another got swept off his horse by a branch … ! The horses bolted for home with stirrups flapping and so we went back to using helicopters.

The recce guys had also come up with another innovation; they took the seats out of a Buffel, laid sandbags in the floor recess and mounted a captured Russian 14.5mm anti-aircraft gun (it might well have been the one from Savate). It was a great idea in that it gave our convoy some comforting firepower. However, it had a few practical shortcomings. It only fired out of one side of the Buffel and it could only fire two or three rounds at a time. Every burst of fire made the whole back section of the Buffel sway back and forwards like a seesaw. The gunners would sit there with stupid grins on their faces waiting for the swaying action to stop so that they could fire another burst.

There was another recce team out there led by Lieutenant Eric Rabie. He was a small guy with a huge heart. His Machilla was almost bigger than he was … how he carried it without it pulling him backwards I could never work out. He had a great sense of humour and a wonderful laugh, but he was seriously pissed off with me by the time he caught up with the convoy. I had been giving him his instructions over the radio for the first few days, sending him seemingly aimlessly all over the place looking for the gooks. What he didn't know was that I was simply relaying these orders from Willem Ratte, who was also out in the bush somewhere. When he stormed up to me standing next to the command Buffel, he let me have it … "Who the fuck do you think you are sending me all over the fucking place … etc, etc?!" I took it on the chin, as I thought it would be really lame to try and blame Willem. I left him to work it out for himself, which I am sure he did.

A few days later, Willem and his small team finally identified a spot where they believed the gooks to be operating from. He instructed me to attack the base in a Buffel mounted cavalry charge! Jolly good idea … I was not into these frontal infantry attacks anymore after Savate! Feeling every bit like Rommel again, I stood in the command Buffel with the rest of the vehicles in line abreast formation to my left and right. Choosing my moment, I gave the imperious command to attack.

With two helicopter gunships circling menacingly above, I desperately tried to manage and co-ordinate the attacking Buffels as they thundered through the bush. It soon degenerated into a shambles as our inexperience in 'armoured attacks' came to the fore. The Buffels had to swerve around the trees and our nice straight extended line became ragged chaos. I soon gave up trying to keep control and hoped for the best, leaving every Buffel for itself. A few of the Browning machine-guns mounted on the Buffels opened up briefly and the gunships overhead fired a few encouraging bursts, but it didn't take long for us to discover that no-one was home … it was a 'lemon'. Maybe this was a good thing as I am sure old 'Rommel' would have had one hell of a time trying to co-ordinate his mechanised force should it have developed into a sizable contact. The only casualty from this escapade was a local 'PB' ('*Plaaslike Bevolking*', the Afrikaans term for local civilian). At the start of our attack, he had taken fright and was shot when he started running back to his kraal, sadly mistaken for an escaping gook. The guerrilla strategy of the 'war of the flea' had worked well for the enemy again as yet another family became irreparably scarred with an enduring hatred of South Africans.

12

A gook comes for tea

Back at the Omauni base, it was at about this time that we had a gook come to tea. We were all sitting in the small *lapa* that was positioned at the centre of the camp, having afternoon tea at about 4 pm. For me, this was one of the highlights of the day. Everyone gathered round, relaxed and took the opportunity to 'chew the fat' over a cup of tea or coffee. A lot of laughs were had as the day's events and jokes were shared. In the middle of this convivial atmosphere, someone said "Hey blokes, check that out … there's a gook!" Looking round, we saw this black guy standing about ten metres away dressed in classic gook kit – AK 47 assault rifle, chest webbing magazines, khaki shirt and Chinese rice pattern trousers, complete with a tatty khaki cap and black chevron soled boots.

We all laughed, thinking it was one of our own troops as they all dressed like that when going into the bush anyway. The banter continued for a while, until everyone suddenly realised that there was a subtle difference with this guy. It suddenly dawned on us all that it was actually a real gook … pandemonium broke out as we all dived for cover, cups and saucers flying! Peering out from our meagre cover, we saw that the gook had quietly collapsed in a heap where he had been standing. Interestingly, the 'big *manne*' who had run the fastest, were the first to pop out of hiding and give him a few kicks and slaps around the head while he sat slumped on the ground, long past posing a threat to anyone. Relieving him of his weapon, we noticed that he was chronically dehydrated and that he hadn't eaten for days.

After sending him off to the medics, we later learned that he was one of a large group of gooks that had tried to reach the farming area to the south. On getting hammered hard in a few contacts, they had started 'bomb-shelling' into smaller groups in an attempt to get back over the border into Angola. Down to just three in his group, they had split up when they ran out of food. He had walked for miles and miles hoping to give himself up before he starved or collapsed from lack of water. On arriving at our base, he had been stopped at the entrance by the engineers tasked with standing guard on top of the water tower. He was relieved only of his bayonet as a trophy, and then told to go on alone (still fully armed) to the middle of the base to surrender! Had he opened fire on us sitting around the tea *lapa*, he would have killed at least five, if not more, of us!

13

The Air Force show

At the beginning of August, I left Rundu with Commandant Ferreira and an Ops Clerk to fly to Oshikati in the west, to prepare for Ops Chaka. I can't be sure of the dates but I think that it was on this trip that we had a very entertaining morning at the big air force base in Oshikati. We had to get some admin done in the morning and then wait for the OC at the air base. He had gone through to the big army base half an hour's drive away at Ondangwa for a briefing with the brass. We arrived there mid-morning and sought out some shade and idly watched the activity on the flight line. We soon noticed that they were preparing two Impala jet fighters, and sure enough, out swaggered two jet-jocks wearing their green g-suits and carrying their bone-dome helmets. They climbed up into their fighters, and the scream of the jet engines spooling up soon changed to that glorious, deep thunderous roar as they rapidly got airborne, heading north at treetop height under a full bomb load. Peace and quiet descended on the air base once more and we settled back to lounge around in our shady spot.

Half an hour later, we suddenly noticed Land Rovers skidding to a halt outside the Ops Room, with the drivers and passengers running into the prefab with much commotion and banging of doors. A few minutes later we saw a lone Impala land, and the pilot quickly ushered into the Ops Room. Not long after, a pair of Alouette gunships got airborne and headed north, followed by a Puma. Still not quite sure what was going on, but nevertheless enjoying the show, we once again settled back so as not to break into a sweat. About an hour later the Puma arrived back and offloaded a very unhappy looking jet-jock. With evident back problems, he was helped along and half carried into the Ops Room. By now we were sitting up and watching with great interest. We couldn't help but see the humour in this … from a suave, swaggering jet jock to a very pained, limping fellow who had to have his bone-dome helmet carried for him!

Our OC arrived soon after and he was quickly ushered into the Ops Room. When he emerged a while later, he filled us in as to what had happened. The Impala had suffered a 'flame-out' on a bombing mission into Angola and the pilot had to eject. We were to join our recce teams at a base to the north of us, and go in with them to blow up the remains of the jet fighter. Suddenly it wasn't so amusing anymore. Thankfully the plan was scrapped later that night. I am sure we would have been dropped straight into a very tight situation as the enemy were bound to have got to the crash site by then.

14

Ops Chaka

Ops Chaka was an operation that saw Willem Ratte badly wounded. I was manning the Tac HQ with Commandant Ferreira from a regular army base at Etale. Willem went in to do a recce to the north of us in southern Angola, in an attempt to pinpoint a large SWAPO base.

I walked out with Willem and his team to board the big Puma standing outside the base. Willem had Sergeant Piet van Eeden with him and two black troops; a medic, Pedro Casomo, and an elderly ex-Angolan army militia member, Filipe Shapata. Willem had captured Filipe in an ambush a few months before and Filipe had opted to return with him and join Three-Two. Filipe claimed there was a large SWAPO base in the area, maintaining that he had relatives living there and he believed they would show them where the base was. Willem was still not sure Filipe could be entirely trusted. They were all very quiet and introspective as they boarded the helicopter, their minds focused on the task that lay ahead of them. The helicopter's twin turbines spooled up and the blades began to spin with their distinctive 'whupp … whupp … whupp … ', lifting off in a cloud of dust before heading north at treetop height. As it was Willem out there, I manned the radios most of the time, making sure we were right on the button with each of his scheduled radio sitreps.

Filipe's intelligence proved correct and Willem and his team soon found scores of SWAPO spoor in the area. They inadvertently found themselves in the middle of the base area as it was getting light on the last morning of the operation. There was very little cover and they concealed themselves as best they could, close to an ant heap. At about mid-morning, a pair of gooks walked passed Willem's patrol. Willem let us know what had happened, by tapping out a morse message over the HF radio. He did not think he and his team had been spotted so they didn't take the precaution of moving, as it was daylight and they were in the middle of a busy base with little cover. In fact, they couldn't move, even if they wanted to! But the gooks *had* seen them, and returned later that afternoon with nearly a hundred men.

The signal to scramble gunships and send in Pumas to lift them out was the Morse code Q for Quebec … da, da, di, da, (here comes the bride…), repeated several times. We were alerted to this that fateful afternoon by a frantic stream of garbled Morse from which Q for Quebec gradually become discernable … a chill went down my spine. It was Willem, and there was obviously a major problem out there. We scrambled everything on cue … but it would take at least twenty minutes for the gunships to get there … and then we waited, trying to guess what had gone wrong.

In the meantime, Willem and his team had opened fire on the attacking gooks. In the opening exchange, Willem was badly wounded in the arm and he dived into the slight depression that housed the radio to call for backup. Seeing Willem was wounded, Piet van Eeden, Filipe and Pedro ran off to the one side and opened fire on the gooks to draw their attention and divert them away from Willem. Filipe and Pedro soon ran out of ammunition and Piet instructed them to break loose and run some 40km to the border. Willem had been battling to hold his own as he was firing only with his right hand as his left arm was badly hit. He then fainted from loss of blood and fell onto the Morse code key, depressing the signal key so we got one long "beeeeeeeeeeeeeeeeeeeee … " coming over the radio.

With the two black guys high-tailing it back to the border, Piet ran back and dived into the depression with Willem to wait for the gunships to arrive. Piet pulled Willem off the Morse key, and started screaming over the radio "Where's the fucking gunships, the gooks have turned and are coming straight for us, *WHERE'S THE FUCKING GUNSHIPS!!?*" The gooks still weren't too sure where they were holed up, but they were now coming straight at them in a long sweep line … he and Willem were simply minutes away from being overrun.

I have never felt so inadequate, as all I could do was lamely assure Piet over the radio that the choppers were on their way. Alone with Willem and almost out of ammunition, it was only the Claymore anti-personnel mines that saved them. Standard operating procedure was for Recce sticks to surround themselves with Claymores when they laid up for the day to rest and sleep (they did their reconnaissance work at night). Piet waited until one gook was right on top of one of his Claymore markers before detonating them … this particular gook was literally cut in half, and several others around him went down too. The gunships got there just as the gooks were recovering and beginning to form up to attack again … and then the turkey shoot began. All in all, over sixteen gooks were accounted for. Close behind the gunships was the Puma with Sergeant Tabo Maree and his team, tasked to evacuate Willem and Piet.

Willem spent the rest of the year with pins sticking out of his left arm to hold it all together… it turned my stomach just to look at them. I often wondered why Piet van Eeden didn't get nominated for the Honoris Crux bravery award. But there again, between Willem and Commandant Ferreira, I think they expected nothing less from their troops. Years later Willem mentioned to me that in hindsight Piet van Eeden well deserved the Honoris Crux … Piet's actions saved not only Willem but the lives of the whole team, and he accounted for most of the enemy killed that day.

I went over the border into Angola with the platoons the next day to attack the base Willem and Piet had discovered. With Alouette helicopter gunships circling protectively, we were trooped in company strength (three platoons), riding with our feet out on the steps of the Puma helicopters to be dropped off in a cloud of black ash. Annoyingly, the Pumas dropped us off-target so we didn't make contact. We advanced line-abreast through the blackened bush, burnt by the fires started from Willem and Piet's contact the day before. Moments after our advance began, the call over the ground-to-air radio came from the leader of the two pairs of Impala strike aircraft streaking in at treetop height …

"Bravo Alpha this is Striker One, do you copy?" Cool, calm and collected in that distinct nasal tone you get through an oxygen mask. "Striker One this is Bravo Alpha go ahead" replied our company commander. "Striker One inbound, five minutes to target, throw yellow smoke". "Roger Striker One, will do," he acknowledged. The yellow smoke grenades were detonated off to the left and right to mark our position and line of advance, and a few minutes later the jets came howling in over us at tree-top height. They held their fire as no targets were being spotted for them by either the ground troops, gunships or the Bosbok circling high above. Each Impala had twin 30mm cannon and racks of ground-to-air rockets slung under their wings, so we had considerable firepower to back us up. It was a classic attack on a guerrilla base and having the Impala jets in support was really cool, the sheer power of their jet engines as they came screaming in made us feel invincible.

With their thunderous roar engulfing us, the Impalas flashed over our heads at treetop height and then banked sharply to the left with their wings just feet away from the trees, to then turnabout and come back in for another run. After their initial 'run-ins', they throttled right back and cruised slowly over us at about a hundred feet. I could clearly see the fighter pilot looking down at me from the cockpit, and couldn't help but waving enthusiastically… he looked back at me like an insect from behind his bone-dome helmet, cool, collected … and with no response. It made me feel a bit foolish. I suppose I should have been focusing ahead of me and making out I was a lean, mean assault troop, but, what the hell!

It turned out that the choppers had dropped us off target, the markers they used for navigation being confused by the previous day's bush fire. So we had zoomed in to attack a very empty, very large, very featureless piece of Angolan bushveld!

I stayed on with one of the platoons trying to locate the gook base. At the end of the first five days, we laid up to wait for the 'rat run'. We carried exactly enough water and food for five days; one water bottle and one rat-pack per day. When it didn't arrive, we were told that all available helicopters were occupied (obviously an attack of some sort somewhere) and to remain where we were. Fortunately I had two cans of tinned fruit squirreled away that I ate at night in the privacy of my slit trench as I didn't want to share them with anyone, savouring every chunk of fruit and every drop of juice. During the day we simply lay in the shade, trying to minimise the loss of moisture from our bodies in the fierce Angolan heat. The Puma only arrived three days later, by which time we had had a troop simply walk off into the bush, delirious from lack of water. Three guys had to run after him and tackle him to the ground, sitting on him and giving him a few *klaps* about the head to subdue him.

Day after day it was the same pleasant routine and the only living thing we saw was a single rabbit that burst from under our feet, zigzagging away like a bat out of hell. We heard a platoon of ours hit contact a good few 'klicks' away, the urgent crackling of automatic rifle fire sounding surreal in our quiet surroundings. The stillness that followed was broken only by the usual post contact radio traffic; reporting their kills, numbers wounded with casevacs required and ammunition and medical resupply requirements. And only once did we have an alarm. Almost midday, we had stopped for a break in our patrol, and I was idly watching two of our burly platoon sergeants under a bush helping each other touch up the 'black-is-beautiful' on their faces. I was thinking how ridiculous they looked, when the alarm was hissed "SWAPO!"… In a flash everything exploded with an electric burst of energy as the sergeants rolled onto their bellies and slithered to their firing positions on the outer fringes of the platoon. The machine gunner who had been sitting with some of his mates to my left and covered about fifteen metres in what seemed like a split second, levitating horizontally a few inches off the ground on his toes and hands as he reached to get his MAG. You could almost hear the air crackling with adrenalin as we waited for the gunfire to explode around us in a welcome release of aggression. But nothing happened, it was a false alarm.

After two or three weeks with the platoon I got a signal from Commandant Ferreira to come back out from the bush and get back to HQ, as another op was being planned. It was with regret that I left the platoon, my newfound home in the endless Angolan bush, having felt accepted and secure within its ranks. The feeling of absolute trust in each other provided a bastion of strength in the sea of a seemingly endless conflict. Already feeling alone, I waited in the tree line listening to the urgency of an approaching Puma, its thudding beat penetrating the air. Crouched over with my Machilla on my back, I ran out into the clearing under the rush of its blades as the re-supply of food and ammunition was being pulled from the craft's hold. Having shrugged off the heavy rucksack, I sat in the door of the chopper and looked out, luxuriating in the rotor wash and enjoying that wonderful weightless feeling. The yellow smoke from the grenade that had guided the Puma in was blasted horizontally away from us by the slipstream as the chopper rose and swivelled towards the south, dropping its nose slightly as it accelerated away just above the trees. It was with a strange empty feeling that I looked back at the platoon, feeling as if I had left a part of my soul out there amongst them, their camouflaged battle fatigues soon rendering them invisible in the dappled tree line.

As it turned out, Willem's trust in Filipe Shapata had been well founded. In recognition of his loyalty, Willem and Commandant Ferreira devised a devious plan to evacuate Filipe's family from Southern Angola. Knowing that they would not get the authority to go back into Angola solely for this purpose, they came up with a cover plan that involved laying landmines in the area. This plan was approved by the brass and Filipe accompanied the recce team that was tasked with this operation. While the mines were being laid, he managed to track his family down in the featureless Angolan bush and, astonished that he was still alive, they readily agreed to be airlifted out of Angola and to accompany Filipe with his new-found career with Three-Two. They went on to join all the other families down at the Buffalo Base in the Caprivi.

15

Rugby in the bush

On getting back to Rundu there was a delay in getting the next field operation under way. Co-incidentally and at this time, the guys down at the training base in Buffalo had this big rugby match planned between two of the companies. One of the platoon commanders got it in his head that I was this dynamite rugby player and organised that I take part, fixing a lift for me on an air force aircraft going down there for the weekend.

I arrived to great excitement, with my teammates practically carrying me on their shoulders as they were absolutely convinced that, with me playing centre in the back line, they would smash the opposing side … as much as I tried to tell them otherwise. It was the hardest, most enjoyable game of rugby I have ever played. The field was an area on the mudflats alongside the Kavango River, with the mud baked to a harsh and unforgiving concrete finish by the merciless sun. Bordered on one side by the broad green river sliding languidly by and the massive reed beds on the other side, the large 'rugby field' itself was devoid of reeds having been flattened by the river and foraging hippos. These huge mammals had left the area crisscrossed with ankle deep indentations, where they had walked whilst the mud was still wet.

Mid-afternoon, wearing just a T-shirt, shorts and takkies (light running shoes) and with a cloudless blue sky above us, the whistle blew for the start. As the rugby ball lofted high towards us, I could see exactly what we were in for. We got hurt in this game whether we were being tackled or doing the tackling. In fact, you got hurt just running across the field as your feet regularly dropped into hippo imprints and down you went, arse over tit. The first injuries were to knees, elbows and hands as the skin flayed off, followed by bruises to various parts of our bodies from the crashing tackles. Whilst we stuck to the 'Queensbury rules' of fair play, by the time the final whistle blew late afternoon, we were exhausted from our magnificent, all out, game of no holds barred rugby.

I can't remember who won, and while I wasn't the great star they had envisioned, I like to think I managed to hold my own. Bloodied and bruised, we had one helluva party that evening in the mess bar, which overlooked our afternoon's 'field of battle' … the river to the left, the 'rugby field' or mudflats in the middle with the reed-beds stretching out to the right and the sun setting golden orange as a backdrop. Surrounded by the timeless sounds of Africa – snorting hippos, the cry of the jackal and the haunting hoot of owls – we had an awesome evening of good cheer and comradeship, accompanied naturally by that golden nectar, Castle Lager. We were young, fit and living our adventure… it was good to be alive and it was good to be a part of Three-Two. We had begun to realize that we were part of an elite and that we were something very unique … and yet, what made us so effective as a fighting unit, was that we carried this with an enduring humility and an unshakable pride.

16

Ops Butterfly

Back in Rundu, I found the planning was getting into full swing for Ops Butterfly and what was to be the first of Ferreira's 'Butterfly Ops'. Being September and the dry season, we targeted a group of wells and waterholes across the border about 40km into Angola. At that time of the year, the gooks had no option but to stick close to them for water supplies. This operation was similar in shape and composition to Savate with three companies, a mortar platoon, and a group of our Recces assigned to the order of battle – the big difference was that in this instance we were heliborne – with about ten Pumas and about sixteen Alouette gunships assigned to us. Indeed, it felt as if every helicopter in the air force had been sent out to us! Getting to Eenhana was interesting as we flew in a Dakota from Oshikati sitting amongst the cargo. This big aircraft flew alarmingly low, at just over a hundred feet the whole way. Some half an hour into the flight, the load master pointed out the window ... tracer bullets were glowing green and red as they eagerly flicked up at us, before floating lazily away above and behind. Luckily the enemy aimed straight at us and by the time their rounds got to where they had aimed, the aircraft had moved on and was long gone. They hadn't allowed for what fighter pilots call 'deflection' ... I wanted to kiss the ground when we landed!

When the attack was launched, the Alouette gunships went ahead, arriving at the Chana Umbi water well to start circling the LZ at about 500 feet with the Pumas coming in low and fast to quickly flare a few feet off the ground and disgorge their troops. The Pumas carried us in to the Landing Zone in three waves, flying ten abreast. It was what I imagined Vietnam to have been like and it was really exhilarating to sit in the open doors of the Puma with our feet on the steps, looking out on either side to see the other choppers flying line abreast at breakneck speed. The HQ element went in on the second wave. As the Pumas settled towards the ground, they would disappear into a mini sandstorm. The pilots must have had to use their instruments to land. There was a light contact on the go just to one side of the *chana* as we hurried to set up the Tac HQ just inside the tree line. I later learned from captured gooks that we had flown straight over an anti-aircraft gun detachment. They had

A gook's-eye view - the belly of an Alouette gunship, its 20mm cannon
just visible sticking out of the left-hand side. This is the view a gook would
have had while the gunship circled above, seeking him out amongst the
trees. Photo by the author while doing a 'camp' with 5 Recce in 1983.

reported the first wave of choppers to their rear command HQ over their HF
radio, asking for permission to open fire when the second wave came in (which
was us). They had been ordered not to open fire, but rather make good their
escape. When it's not your time, it's not your time!!

There were several water holes in the surrounding area and over the next
few days we used the Butterfly Ops concept that Ferreira had devised. There
were about eight waterholes within twenty minutes flying time of us. Selecting
each in turn, we would send in the slower Alouette gunships so they would
get to the waterhole, just as the Pumas arrived to offload the Three-Two troops.
With our troops advancing shoulder-to-shoulder and in open order from two
sides of the *chana*, the gunships would circle menacingly above with their
20mm cannons at the ready. The insurgents would be flushed out from their
meagre cover and killed by the ensuing air and ground fusillade.

Once the skirmish at the waterhole was over, the bodies would be counted
and searched for intel, and the weapons and ammunition collected. Our troops
would reload their magazines from the Pumas and while taking a breather,
would have a quick bite of a dog biscuit and a drink of water... ready for

The deadly 20mm cannon, on this occasion in a Rhodesian 'K-car'. (Courtesy of Max T.)

the next 'Butterfly'. By this time the gooks that had escaped from the first waterhole, would have run frantically through the bush, arriving at the next one. The fact was that they had no option but to head for them, in that they had to get to the next waterhole in order to make it out of there. The Alouette gunships would by then have refuelled as well and would set off to get to the next waterhole being targeted, again timing it to arrive at the same time as the Pumas did to disgorge their troops. And once again the advancing troops together with the Alouette gunships circling above would begin their deadly work, using the same coordinated tactics as before.

And so we moved from waterhole to waterhole in the first three days. It was a turkey shoot, killing eighty-four gooks and capturing six in the first three days. Losses on our side amounted to just one dead and three wounded. These casualties were the result of a friendly fire incident when one of our Alouette gunships mistook some Three-Two soldiers for gooks. Other than this unfortunate incident, Butterfly Ops had worked like clockwork. We even had the legendary Neall Ellis arrive, clattering in over the trees in his Alouette gunship, unannounced, and literally out of the blue. He had heard that there was good shooting to be had with Three-Two at Chana Umbi, and he didn't want to be left out of the action!

On the morning of the second day, someone went to get water from the well in the middle of the *chana*. When they cranked the handle up, much to their surprise, they discovered a young boy sitting in the bucket that had been suspended at the bottom of the well shaft. The day before, when the Alouette gunships had arrived overhead, the boy had shimmied down the well as there was nowhere else to hide. They never found his parents and he came back with us when we returned to our side of the border. One of our black troops adopted him as his son and he went on to live with his adoptive family at the Buffalo training base. The first night back at an army base on our side of the border, I noticed him staring unblinkingly at the electric light bulb suspended from the Command Bunker's roof … absolutely mesmerised. It took me a while to realise he had never seen a light bulb before.

The next day, we got word of a small group of gooks located someway off to the east and we dispatched the Alouette gunships and, a little later, some Pumas with troops. Gav Veenstra was with them and during the ensuing firefight they killed about six gooks and captured four of them. It turned out to be their HQ group. It was sobering to discover that two of the dead were women, armed and in uniform. They radioed back to say that they had captured some signallers with their radios intact. I met the choppers as they came roaring back to land in the *chana* late that afternoon. To my surprise it turned out to be none other than my counterpart … Commander Hindongo, Commander in Chief of Communications for that sector together with his signaller! He certainly outranked me with this grand title, but on the ground we were pretty much on a par! I initially wondered if I should do any of the chivalrous things that I had read about when fellow officers met under these circumstances, but then I quickly realised that it would be a little inappropriate. Trained as a guerrilla fighter in the Ukraine, he very obviously hadn't done the 'Officer as a Gentleman' as part of his training! So our troops dug a pit (two metres square by a metre high) in the middle of our camp, covered it with a mesh of wooden poles and unceremoniously bundled the Commander and his colleagues into it. We placed two guards over them.

I had a careful look at their Russian radios and couldn't make much headway as to how to get them working. So we pulled the signaller out of the pit, and, giving him a good few persuasive blows to the head, instructed him to fire up the radio. This he did with great alacrity. Spurred on by our success, we then told him to contact his mates and tell them to meet him and his group at a specific time and rendezvous point – where of course we would be waiting in covert ambush. This he cottoned onto and he suddenly started to find difficulty with his radio … more blows, this time with a rifle butt or two. The devilish signaller got the better of us though and the radio suddenly 'shorted itself out'. By now I could see the comedy in this and I had begun to feel a grudging respect for him. His actions earned him a good beating from the others and he was dumped head first back into the pit.

Each night, all the choppers would fly back across the border into the safety of South West Africa, arriving back the next day soon after dawn. On one of the days the Pumas were trooping our guys into an area around one of the waterholes, an aircraft got hit in both the tail section and tail rotor. The pilot conducted an emergency and landed in a *chana* while the gunships circled protectively above. The technicians simply took off the entire tail section and brought it back to Chana Umbi, sticking out either side of the open doors of another Puma. A new one arrived the next day and they bolted it on and took off again. Later that same day the air force put on an awesome show for us … it was like watching a huge family of dragon flies escorting their wounded home. The Alouette gunships took off first and circled the *chana*, test firing their 20mm canons. Then the Pumas lifted off, one of which had the damaged tail section protruding through its open doors, and another lifted off with an entire unserviceable Alouette helicopter suspended beneath it. They had merely removed the rotor blades and attached a rope to the 'Jesus nut'. With a thunderous roar that engulfed us, and seemed to fill the heavens from horizon to horizon, over twenty helicopters then headed south, with the Alouette gunships circling protectively around the Pumas in the middle. The silence was deafening when they disappeared over the horizon heading south. With the sun setting gently in the west, we were left to our whispered conversations and the inky black African night.

I was hugely impressed the one day to see a four-barrelled, hydraulically operated machine-gun mounted in one of the Alouette gunships. If I remember correctly they might well have been belt-fed, water-cooled Vickers machine-guns of World War One vintage! This was instead of the usual 20mm cannon. The engineer-gunner merely moved two small handgrips connected to a gun-sight and the barrels followed. They test fired it after lifting off and the rate of

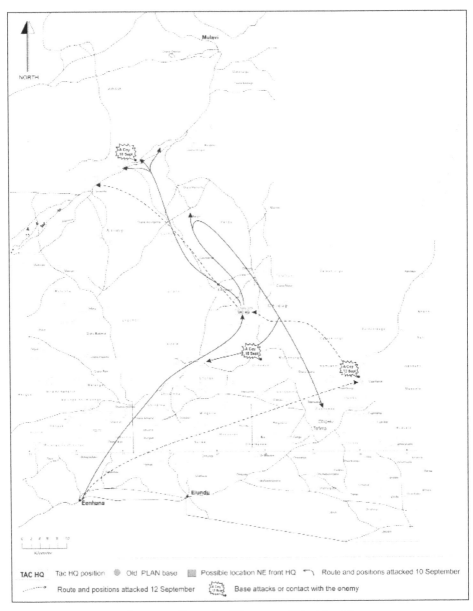

Operation Butterfly. (Courtesy of Piet Nortje)

The delightful young lady who kept us company in the command bunker and from whom
we drew a great deal of inspiration. She was unanimously crowned 'Miss Umbi 1980'

fire was unbelievable … the sound was something akin to the roaring, frantic
tearing of a cotton shirt. The bush he aimed at simply disappeared in a cloud
of dust. Incredible! We were absolutely convinced this would win the war for
us! Yet we later heard they went back to using the 20mm cannon. The gooks
weren't as scared of the multi-barrelled machine-guns as they were of the 20
mil … the ripping crackle of the multiple machine-guns didn't frighten them
as much as the boom of the single-barrelled cannon and as a result, they stood
their ground and shot back against the machine-guns.

We stayed on in the bush for over a month, chasing the spoor of gooks
and their shadows. The pin-up that kept us company in the command bunker
is pictured above – Commandant Ferreira's signature heads the list, which is
followed by that of the 'MAYOT' or the air force liaison officer, mine, Corporal
John Bodley, the Command Bunker Signaller, others and then the docs at
the bottom. Ferreira played endless games of bridge with the chopper pilots,
sitting in the main bunker that had all the radios and maps in it. It measured
about three metres by four and two metres deep, with a third of the bunker

covered by poles and sand bags. The OC and pilots used a big ammo case filled with mortar bombs as their card table and the smaller cases of small arms ammunition as chairs. This coupled with all the ordnance lying around and its large open design meant I was not sure how effective the bunker would have been had an enemy mortar landed in it, hence my plan was to be sure I wasn't in there if we got attacked, unless it was absolutely necessary. When things got really boring I remember Ferreira putting a dollop of jam on the ammo case, and then waiting to see how many flies he could attract into his 'killing field'. When he judged there was the maximum number of flies possible in the killing field, he would smash down the fly swatter, counting with glee the number of flies he had killed in one go. I read some years later how he had used this very same tactic at the Battle of the Lomba River in Angola, where he had lured an entire FAPLA division into his chosen killing field before annihilating them with artillery fire.

A signal came in from our rear Tac HQ at Eenhana that there had been a fight between our black troops and the Parabats. This caused a lot of concern initially, until the details came through later. A Parabat had picked a fight with one of our lightly wounded guys and was quickly joined by his mates in support, at which the rest of our wounded and sick piled out of their tents and into the fight with their legs, arms and heads swathed in plaster casts and bandages. The best part of this was that they saw the Parabats off. Commandant Ferreira laughed about that for days … our 'sick, lame and lazy' getting the better of the tough and elite Parabats! I never quiet understood the animosity between the Parabats and Three-Two, but maybe it was something to do with our respective kill ratios. If I remember correctly, the 'Bats had about 100 kills in that year with 35 of their own dead, whereas we sustained about the same dead with some 700 kills achieved. Maybe that was what pissed them off so much? Thing was, it was an unfair comparison as they were used as fire-force or hot pursuit operations most of the time, and as such continuously ran into ambushes. Three-Two on the other hand invariably took their time and chose their fights with care.

I spent many an evening sitting on the lip of a trench overlooking the *chana* and talking to Sergeant Gavin Veenstra. With the sun setting off to our right, and sipping a hot fire-bucket of tea, we covered many a topic and had some good laughs. He came from a farm in Mooi River and had grown up with my girlfriend, so we had plenty in common and a lot to talk about. He was a tall, well-built and good-looking guy with curly blond hair. He had the mark of an excellent soldier – mentally and physically strong and as brave as a lion, all of which was balanced by a deep compassion for his fellow man. He usually covered up this compassionate side when around the other tough guys in the recce wing with his easy smile and infectious laugh. For me, he was one of the guys that represented the quintessential soldier … strength, bravery, compassion. It was the guys that had little or no compassion that I didn't want alongside me in a firefight. They were generally unpredictable and I felt that I couldn't rely upon them when the chips were down, especially if things turned against us. I would have had 'Gawie' Veenstra alongside me any time. He died some years later, hunting down a group of renegade black guys who had robbed the farm next to his back home in South Africa. A fluke pistol shot from over eighty metres hit him in the heart. (Gawie was pronounced 'Gggavie' with the Afrikaans guttural, rolling G and a V for the W).

Gawie also reminded me a lot of his friend in the recce group, Sergeant Gavin 'Gav' Monn. Being a big strong guy, he was of similar build and character. However, what set them apart was that Gav was often called on to perform the role of company commander, a position usually assigned to a Captain. I think the reason he wasn't made an officer was because he had a wonderfully straight way of putting his views across – he wouldn't suffer fools and wasn't intimidated by rank. He also had a refreshingly straight, frank manner and way in which he dealt with his troops.

We were mortared one night … that spine chilling cough of the big 82mm mortar bombs leaving their tubes just over a kilometre away, followed a few seconds later by the frightening rush of air from the bombs coming down on us, and then the cruummp, cruummp, cruummp as they exploded nearby, seeking out our positions in the night. We had great expectations of some guys with us, who were trying some new fangled triangulation system that would give us the exact direction and distance of the enemy mortars, enabling our own mortars to respond and annihilate them with pinpoint accuracy. We were impressed by this technology and accorded them a certain amount of respect as a result. However, when it came down to the wire, as it were, it didn't work very well. I think they had slackened from waiting around for weeks in the bush, as when the real thing finally happened they ran around reconnecting wires and things, becoming increasingly flustered and in the process losing the 'Golden Moment' they had been waiting so long for. Unable to delay any longer while they sorted themselves out, we opened up with our own 81mm mortars in the general direction of the enemy. With a 'thoomp–thoomp … thoomp–

thoomp' that hurt your ears and reverberated in your chest, our two mortar tubes, just a few metres away from the HQ, began firing a spread pattern, dropping the bombs over the area from which the enemy were shooting at us. This mortar duel continued for about twenty minutes when suddenly the enemy mortars fell silent.

When the excitement had died down, I unlaced my boots and slid fully clothed into my sleeping bag at the bottom of my slit trench. With the comfort of my rifle next to me, I thought back over the evening's events. Gazing up at the stars, I felt a huge dose of admiration for these gooks, or more respectfully, these SWAPO guerrillas. Despite having taken a thrashing from our heli-borne troops and gunships over the past few days, they still had the courage and tenacity to come back close enough to get within mortar range…. knowing full well that we would send out our Alouette gunships first thing in the morning to seek and destroy them. Having fired at us early in the evening, they would immediately have started their escape and evasion process, running for the rest of the night, carrying the heavy base plates, mortar tubes and any remaining bombs with them. Spurring them on was the knowledge that if they didn't cover enough ground before the sun rose, we would catch up with them and their fate would be sealed. Even with these odds against them, they still had the courage and tenacity to give it a go. This particular group's élan paid off as we lost their spoor midday from a breeze which started mid-morning and blew lightly through the bush, covering their tracks in the soft white sand.

We lived in our slit trenches on the edge of Chana Umbi for over a month with no showers. Ablutions were gentle strolls out into the bush with toilet paper and an entrenching tool in hand. We were nearly driven mad by the flies. Our combat fatigues had long since been caked stiff with dirt on our thighs and backs. If you tried to bend the material it simply cracked. Boy, did we get pissed when we finally got out of Angola and back to the base at Eenhana!

We moved into groups scattered about the *chana* roughly two hundred metres apart and the Pumas came in waves to take us out, pretty much as we had come in. The junior element of the HQ was near the end, as we kept the Tac HQ comms open using HF radios in case of any incidents that required co-ordination. It was a long day, watching the Pumas coming in, each loading about ten troops with all their kit and then disappearing south. Finally it was our turn. For a good few minutes before we saw them, we heard the unmistakable thud of their approaching rotor blades and then suddenly they broke into view just inches above the tree line, each Puma heading for its allotted group.

Ours flared about a hundred feet above us and a hundred metres ahead, before descending and disappearing into its own mini sandstorm. Even before the dust had started settling, we began jogging towards the chopper, Machilla rucksacks on our backs, rifles in one hand and carrying the cases of comms equipment slung between two of us. The big Puma slowly became visible through the murk and with the roar of the blades above, we slung the cases up onto the floor of the cabin. Climbing up, we turned and, shrugging off our Machillas, we sat facing out the door with our feet outside on the step and our rifles held across out laps. We felt the chopper lift off as the pitch of the blades changed and we rose up into the blinding sand storm. Suddenly breaking out of the dust cloud, we had a panoramic view of Chana Umbi, our home for over a month. Perhaps five square kilometres of open ground with the water well in the middle, it was fringed with the dry, brown bush that stretched away, flat and featureless to the horizon. And there just in the tree line was our trusty, fly-infested Temporary Base. Clearly visible in the white sand between the scraggly trees were the command bunker and mortar pits, encircled by the slit trenches of the HQ protection platoon, our recent occupancy evidenced by the sand still freshly churned by our boot prints.

The Puma nosed over, and turning to the south accelerated into a ragged line abreast formation with the other Pumas just above the treetops. Twenty minutes later we flashed out of Angola, back over the cut-line towards the regular army base at Eenhana eagerly anticipating hot showers, massive mess-cooked meals and ice-cold beers. There was a white infantry Major just up from South Africa in charge of the base. He was the real deal, regular Army with snappy salutes, short back and sides, shining boots and perfectly ironed combat fatigues. As much as he tried not to show it, his nose was seriously put out of joint when this unruly mob arrived on his doorstep; wild disheveled hair, unshaven black faces streaked with sweat, with hints of white skin appearing through the 'black-is-beautiful', rumpled and filthy camouflaged combat fatigues and worst of all … unpolished boots. And being armed to the teeth with a variety of weapons, mostly stuff the gooks would carry, just didn't do it for him. And of course the irony was that he failed to notice the one thing that really was of any relevance… the immaculate state of our weaponry, the relaxed discipline amongst us and the easy manner with which we moved about the bush.

In all his wisdom he allowed the HQ element into the base, but not the companies. There were mutterings that this white Major did not want Three-

Two in his base because of our black troops. He sent beers out to the platoon leaders as a conciliatory gesture. Big mistake … after a few beers out in the bush that night, and being pissed off about the perceived racial slur against their troops, the white officers and NCOs started firing machine gun rounds and RPGs over the base. With RPGs detonating above him and tracers curving gracefully across his camp, the regular Army Major went berserk. He went rushing around, throwing everything that had anything to do with 32 Battalion out of his base. He then went *completely* apeshit on seeing how pissed we were when he came to throw out the junior element of the HQ. To add insult to injury, we hadn't bothered to have a shower or attempt to clean ourselves up before we had started joyfully smashing beers in our faces. Loaded up with all our kit, it took us several attempts to get up and over the embankment that surrounded the base. There was much shouting and hilarity as our heavy Machillas pulled us backwards down the bank as we lost our balance. We finally made it, pushing and pulling each other over the wall, only to tumble down the other side in a jumble of backpacks, rifles, and flailing limbs before ending up in the bushes. It really wasn't very sporting of the Major at all.

Gathering ourselves together in the dark, we dusted ourselves off and I got everyone into an extended line and we heroically began our advance towards the landing strip. Any semblance of order soon degenerated as we staggered along, bleary eyed and with our ears ringing from the over-abundance of beers we had consumed. Weaving our way over the starlit airfield and moving about forty metres into the bush on the other side, I hastily steered everyone into a rough circle before they collapsed onto the sand. I then stumbled from one to the next telling each what time their guard duty was. Only after a good few kicks could I would get any semblance of a grunted acknowledgement, not that I was in much better shape.

Even after my cajoling to ensure they would all stand their shift at the appropriate time, dawn revealed all eight of our bodies scattered unceremoniously about, each snoring loudly amongst an untidy jumble of kit. Had the guerrillas found us that night – and we hadn't been snoring so loudly – they might well have left us for dead. As the scorching sun rose mercilessly, the heat dried our tongues and alcohol-soused perspiration began running down our faces. But it was the squadrons of flies that woke us, alighting with delight on our upturned faces and open mouths. We faced a long day with terrible *babalases* (hangovers) making our heads throb and our eyeballs ache.

However, the real party was about two weeks later in Ruacana. When we left Chana Umbi, some of the companies had patrolled across to the west, coming back across the border from Angola at Ruacana. We had one hell of a party that night in a command bunker they had converted into an impromptu pub next to the big airfield. We were celebrating being alive, being part of Three-Two and our macabre success… we had killed 83 of the enemy. Sometime after midnight, I was unexpectedly informed that my Signals team and I were to leave with the OC at dawn to set up a Tac HQ just off to the east. Now trying to sober up, we stumbled around, still pissed but trying not to let our 'inebriated ineptitude' hinder the task at hand. We somehow collected our signals gear together before curling up to sleep alongside our kit. We even managed to get ourselves to the big Puma in the dark before first light and get it loaded with all our kit by the time the OC and the chopper pilots ambled out. We mumbled good morning through bloodshot eyes as the sun cracked over the distant horizon and the dawn broke fresh and crisp around us. As the chopper rose with its blades thudding into the cool air, we welcomed the blast of the wind in our faces as having had only a couple of hours' sleep, I think we were still a bit pissed.

That was the flight that roared low across a *chana* and straight over a farmer tilling his field with a donkey. Sitting with my feet out the door and wedged on the step, I looked back to see the donkey galloping wildly across the furrows with the farmer being dragged behind. He was trying desperately to hang onto the plough. He eventually had to let go and he disappeared in a cloud of dust as the donkey bolted off into the bush with the plough bouncing madly behind it. I lost sight of them as we skimmed away, ten feet off the ground.

Having set up the new Tac HQ, we then sat in some nondescript army base right on the cut-line, with a pair of gunships on standby, ready to support some platoons we had in Angola just north of us. It wasn't particularly successful. We returned to Rundu after about two weeks. It was to be my last Op.

17

Training the Signallers

I now had 'min days' until my National Service was up at the end of the year and so we started the process of training the troops coming in to replace us. The first course saw us training the new Signaller intake. This I did from Omauni, out to the west of Rundu where the Reconnaissance wing commanded by Willem Ratte was based. Willem and his guys threw themselves wholeheartedly into this exercise, without which it would not have been the success and fun that it was.

I took the initiative of putting this course together in order to prepare the Signallers for any eventuality they might find themselves in with their time at Three-Two. It was motivated by my experiences on arriving at the Battalion little prepared for what lay ahead. It was a two week programme, the first half being combat infantry orientation with bush-fighting techniques, followed by a week of signals training with the emphasis being on the development of hands-on, practical, signalling skills. Fresh from the training camps back in South Africa, I loaded the skittish and wary new Signallers into Buffels and trooped them in a small convoy from Rundu to Omauni. I made a point of informing them we were heading west, and as such we were going into Sector One Zero, in which guerrilla activity was a lot more prolific then Sector Two Zero – where Rundu was located. Added to this, Willem Ratte and his guys had prepared a welcome party that was designed to introduce the rookie Signallers to the real Three-Two and give them a good natured *skrik* (Afrikaans for 'fright'). Suffice to say, Willem ended up scaring the shit out of me as well!

Strapped securely into our harnesses, sitting back to back and facing out over the sides of our Buffels we arrived a few kilometres from the base just as it was getting dark. The bush alongside the dirt road had begun to look increasingly ominous. Unbeknown to us, a trip wire had been stretched across the road which set off a bunch of flares. Whooshing over our heads, the booby trap then automatically triggered a whole case of PE4 plastic explosives buried alongside the road. An earth-shattering explosion that sucked the air from our lungs blew a crater big enough to stand in just a few metres from the road, showering us in the Buffels with clods of dirt. The Signallers had hardly

Signallers' Course - Home-sweet-home for the troops. They are pictured dug
in to their slit trenches in which they lived for the duration of the course.

Signallers' Course - Gav Veenstra throwing a hand-grenade
with Corporal John van Dyk looking on.

Signallers' Course - Corporal Grant Larkin, the Ops Medic,
taking it easy. Note the AK-47s lying around.

Signallers' Course - Sergeant Gav Veenstra instructing
on the Russian AK-47, AKM and RPK.

gathered themselves from this when we swept into the base, to be greeted in the gathering dusk by a scene reminiscent of the movie, *Apocalypse Now*. Willem's wild bunch were all dressed up as fanatical gooks, bedecked with bayonets, hand-grenades, pistols, AK-47s and glistening machine gun belts draped over their shoulders, some complete with big Afro wigs and 'black-is-beautiful' smeared across their faces. By this stage, the Signallers eyes were as wide as saucers, peering down from up on the Buffels thinking that we may have inadvertently driven into an enemy-held base.

The 'commanders' of this unruly mob were dressed in a similar fashion, their true identity being hardly recognizable. But they were none other than the flamboyant 'Commandante' Eric Rabie, who, being barely five feet tall, was dwarfed by his 'Adjutant', Willem Ratte, who towered over him at well over six feet tall. Led by these dubious, tatty-looking commanders, the unruly mob started screaming at the Signallers to get down from the Buffels and when they understandably hesitated, a few AK-47 rounds were fired into the air above them. This had them debussing with alacrity, falling over each other in their panic to form up. They were then unceremoniously frog marched into the corrugated iron mess hall and screamed at to lie prone on the bare concrete, where one of the circling hooligans would scream "GET UP YOU STUPID MOTHER FUCKER WHITEY....." followed shortly by "WHO THE FUCK TOLD YOU TO STAND UP YOU USELESS POES.... LIE DOWN!" They were then hauled up four at a time to be tried on various charges before the comic pair of 'Commanders', Commandante Eric and his bumbling Adjutant Willem. Behind Willem and Eric and facing the terrified Signallers, in such a way that they couldn't miss it, was the Situation Board:

Battle Situation				
	Killed	**Wounded**	**Prisoners**	**Missing**
Enemy Forces	2	5	0	0
Own Forces	58	93	22	13

Hospital Situation					
Malaria	**Syphilis & VD**	**Gunshot wounds**	**Amputations**	**Gangrene**	**Mentally Discharged**
90	64	19	9	26	8

With each batch of Signallers being found guilty of various crimes by the inept pair of 'commanders' who kept interrupting, confusing and contradicting each other, the Signallers were dragged outside into the darkness.

This would be followed by thumps and thwacks followed by screams of mercy. Unbeknown to those remaining in the mess hall, the 'wretched' Signallers who had been dragged outside were already in the pub with beers in hand and confused, bewildered expressions on their faces. The special effects of thwacking, thumping and screaming was the handy-work of some of Willems' bunch, who were trying desperately not to laugh in the process. Whilst back inside the mess hall, chaos continued to reign as each zombie continued to give contradictory orders and the two useless 'commanders' vainly tried to stamp their authority.

All of this was handled superbly by Willem and his guys, confusing and scaring the hell out of the Signallers without taking it too far. Although they eventually saw the funny side of it, I noticed that we had rattled them to the extent that they forever recounted their experiences of that evening with fleeting, tight smiles. Their terror had been genuine... and we had achieved what we'd set out to do.

Next morning we issued them with fresh ammunition and after checking their weapons, took them out to the north and set up a TB in the bush, close to the Angolan border. We had the Signallers dig in to form a circular perimeter, with the Tac HQ and 60mm mortar pit in the middle. Here we put them through a basic combat orientation course. Willem had given me three of his top recce group guys as instructors – sergeants Gav Veenstra, Tabo Maree and 'Daisy' Loubscher. We introduced all the course students to a range of Russian and Eastern Bloc weapons as well as the NATO weapons we used. They were lectured on their inner workings and fired them all on the bush range. We did a lot of fire and movement drills with the standard R1 assault rifles, all with live ammunition. Towards the end of the week I made a point of having them experience the sensation of live rounds cracking over their heads. During a short patrol, we went down in a small depression and then, issuing instructions over a VHF radio, we had a machine gun together with a few assault rifles fire over our heads. For the whole week, they had lived with their faces and hands covered in 'black-is-beautiful', applying the cream every morning to ensure we couldn't see their white skin. They slept each night in slit trenches, ate rat-packs and drank warm water from their water bottles.

I briefed them each morning outside my 'command centre', an army tent we used as the Tac HQ with radios, maps... the works. I would explain to them what they were to do that day with regards to combat training and then gave them a fictitious intelligence briefing. To this end, I had left a series of 'daily

Signallers' Course - Sgt Tabo Maree instructing on the Russian PKM machine gun. Initially designed for use mounted on a tank, it was also used as an infantry support weapon.

Signallers' Course - Sgt Gavin Veenstra instructing on the NATO Bren Gun.

intelligence events' back at Omauni, so that they would be radioed through to us each morning and decoded by one of the Signallers on the course. They each took turns to man the radios in the Tac HQ as part of their training. So with them hearing it firsthand over the radio, they took it as the real thing. The scenario I had created was one in which there was a large build-up of enemy forces to the north-west of us and there had been heavy battles fought with plenty of casualties on both sides. According to my 'intelligence', things were not looking good at all.

At the end of the week when the combat orientation course had conveniently come to an end, Willem Ratte and three of his men 'reconned' our base overnight wearing the distinctive chevron soled boots favoured by gooks. This was discovered by our daily security patrol comprised of one of the Signals teams, who returned to the TB with great alacrity. They made their report with wide eyes and anxious glances over their shoulders... the surrounding bush had suddenly taken on an air of menace that hadn't been there earlier. I then radioed Omauni to report our predicament and to request back up, making sure that some of the Signallers were within earshot. The primed response was short and sweet ... with the action going on to the NW they had their hands

Signallers' Course - Sgt Tabo Maree firing the Russian Dragunov
sniper rifle and the Russian RPG-7 anti-tank rocket launcher.

Signallers' Course – Fire and movement with live ammunition.

full and we were therefore on our own. After some careful 'deliberation', I gathered the troops around me. Having been in the bush for a week, I was faced with a bunch of filthy, scruffy Signallers, all with very anxious black faces from which round white eyes peered at me. Drawing myself up to begin my speech, I squared my shoulders and looked them in the eye, feeling every bit like General Montgomery addressing his troops before the Battle of El Alamein … I began my address;

"Men, over the past week we have received sitreps from Omauni, informing us of larger than normal groups of gooks attacking an outlying army base. In the ensuing follow-up action, a large number of our troops from Omauni were required to support the regular army engaged with the enemy. The fighting has been significant and we have suffered serious casualties. There are no spare troops available to come to our assistance and we have been informed that it is too dangerous to attempt to make it back to Omauni….. we are on our own." Pausing dramatically, I allowed all this to sink in.

"Given that we are Three-Two Battalion, and even though we haven't quite completed our training, I feel that we have no option but to follow up the spoor in the true fighting spirit of the Battalion. Our credo is Latin for 'Forged in

Battle'. Let's hope that you as rookie Signallers will have the opportunity and honour of being forged in battle in the true tradition of the Battalion. Given your calibre and the quality of the combat training you have just received, I have absolutely no doubt that we will more than hold our own and, in fact, acquit ourselves well in the task ahead." By now some eyes had grown even wider, others were fidgeting and some were scratching their heads... I could just imagine what they were thinking.

"Our mission is to aggressively follow up on the spoor in order to identify the size and composition of the enemy. This will give me the information I need in order to make a plan of attack." A few Adams apples bobbed up and down with that one.

I selected the two strongest and most capable Signallers as the machine gunners, issuing one with a MAG and the other a Russian PKM. With only about fifteen of us making up the platoon, I split them into two sections, with Shaun Prior as the 60 mil mortar man and one of the Signallers as my radio man. And of course, I was the platoon commander ... finally! We walked in a square U with the open end behind us and the machine-guns out to the front corners. We briefly rehearsed the flat sections of the square U swinging around to form into a line abreast, ready to advance and we then set off on the spoor. The chevron-soled boots worn by Willem and his team were clear in the white sand, heading in a northwesterly direction. Their 'spoor' led us by the end of the day to the edge of a large, open *chana*.

That night we used an 'abandoned' enemy TB that had been set up by Willem and his guys. We dug in carefully within its perimeter and placed our 60 mil mortar pit in the middle. We had to be exactly positioned for what was to happen next. Willem's guys started their 'attack' at about 9 pm, mortaring us from the other side of the *chana* with the big 81mms. The sound of the mortar bombs firing from their tubes just over a kilometre away, with their distinctive low 'cough', never failed to raise the hairs on the back of my neck. I instinctively held my breath as I knew the bombs were on their way, soon followed by the rushing of air from the mortar rounds coming down above us and the distinct 'Ka-boom... ka-boom' as they detonated against the ground.

With the bombs creeping ever closer, I kept up a constant commentary to my troops as they lay in their trenches, telling them it was the gooks attacking us and explaining what I would be expecting of them in retaliation. The last thing I needed was one of them to panic and jump out of a trench. The mortar bombardment lasted about 20 minutes, with the closest bombs falling barely

Signallers' Course – Sergeant Gavin Veenstra (Recce
Instructor) cleaning the HK21 machine gun.

Signallers' Course – Getting ready for the night security
patrol - Signalmen Kempkin-Smith, Mann, de Wet.

30 metres away … a bit closer than I had anticipated! Some of the bombs exploded in the trees, and a chunk of shrapnel whizzed down into Corporal Shaun Prior's 60mm mortar pit, missing him by just a few centimetres. Willem was doing the fire control, hidden in the dark a couple of hundred metres behind us. If he and the mortar guy had a devilish plot to scare the shit out of us, it certainly worked! It was no surprise at top marks for Willem's fire control and the accuracy of the mortar team.

Willem then set off an 'automatic' ambush from out in the *chana*. Several machine-guns strapped to the ground had elastic bands around their triggers, held off by a piece of string. When a fuse was lit on the one end, it burnt through the string, the elastic bands would contract on the trigger and the machine-gun would fire through its ammunition belt. These fired long bursts into the branches over our heads, but with some of the guns coming loose from their mountings, instead of the rounds going through the trees, they shredded the bushes just inches above our heads. I was very proud of my Signallers, who all stayed calm, firing controlled bursts back at the 'enemy' only when instructed to. I was particularly pleased when L/Cpl Buys, one of the rookie machine gunners lying in a trench next to me, fired bursts of three or four rounds at a time from his MAG just as we had taught him to. This conserved his supply of ammunition and helped maintained a semblance of accuracy with the recoil of the MAG hammering back into his shoulder.

There were three Permanent Force guys with us, 2nd Lieutenant MacMillan (of Irish descent) and two corporals from the Signals School back in Heidelburg, South Africa. MacMillan acquitted himself well 'under fire', whilst the two corporals cowered in their slit trenches – one not firing a single round in retaliation and the other not daring to stick his head out of his trench, choosing rather to lift his rifle up and blindly fire off into the dark. These two guys were very much feared back at camp. During 'Basics' at the beginning of our military training, they had actually gone as far as pushing their respective platoons so hard that two or three of their troops had died of over-exertion. Tough guys … until faced with the real thing. I considered writing a report, especially on hearing that they had arrived back at Heidelburg to swagger around the base, boasting about having been trained by 'the Recces' on the border. Interestingly, the remake of the movie *All Quiet on the Western Front* about some German soldiers in World War One portrays a similar story.

The Signallers spent a very anxious night without much sleep. In the morning, under the ruse that we were outgunned and outnumbered, we

Signals Theory, Omauni, 32 Battalion Reconnaissance Base - Corporal
Prior, Signalman Base, Signalman Pitschlitz, Corporal Bodley, Signalman
Wessels, Corporal Price, Signalman de Wet, Signalman Kirschof, Signalman
Knoetze, Signalman Kemkin-Smith, Signalman Mann.

moved back to the temporary training base we had set out from the day
before. Most of them had run out of water by mid-morning and the strain was
beginning to show clearly on their faces during this retreat. With barely five
kilometres to go, we heard a short sharp contact flare up immediately ahead
of us, directly in the area of our base. Arriving about an hour later, we moved
into an extended line and advanced, sweeping slowly through what was left of
our base. There were signs of a hasty retreat from the five or six men we had
left there and the camp had been looted. I could see from the nervous glances
and whispered conversations that the rookie Signallers were nearing the end of
their tether. We moved to the nearby water hole and I got them to move into
a protective circle, with each troop taking it in turn individually to come in
and fill his water bottle. Those on the perimeter squatted quietly in the sand,
staring intently into the surrounding bush, searching for the elusive enemy
and expecting an attack at any moment. I suddenly noticed a second troop at
the waterhole and recognized him as one of the 'hero instructors' from back in
South Africa.

Signals Theory, Omauni, 32 Battalion Reconnaissance Base, Lecture
Room - Signalman Base (second left), Signalman Knoetze (right).

32 Battalion Signals Course, Final Selection - The first team makes it back
the following day to the rendezvous point with great relief - Corporal
Bodley, Signalman Kempkin-Smith, Signalman Kirshov.

32 Battalion Signals Course, Final Selection - One of the
teams head off on their assigned tasks for the night.

When I asked him what he was doing there he replied, "I'm thirsty Lieutenant" with a whining, insolent expression on his face. In a rare flash of anger I said "Pour that water out, get the fuck back to your position and wait your turn". We stared each other out for a while before he finally dropped his gaze and pouring the water out, slunk back to his position on the waterhole's perimeter.

Once they had all refilled their water bottles, I sat alongside the waterhole and watched them carefully. After about half an hour, I saw them begin to visibly relax a little. Calling them all in together, they looked at me as if I had gone mad. What was I doing making them abandon their positions and bunch up in a group when the enemy were rampaging like elusive ghosts all around us. It was then that I informed them that it was all a hoax, letting them in on the fact that it had all been staged. I was met with incredulous, blank stares and it took a while to sink in ... this was then followed by huge relief and much nervous laughter. They then stopped and looked at me suspiciously, carefully checking that I wasn't pulling the wool over their eyes again. It was only after they had thought it all through a few times that they really relaxed and started ribbing each other mercilessly. It was very interesting to see how

32 Battalion Signals Course, Final Selection - troops happy to be getting
water from the built-in tank under the Buffel, Corporal John Bodley in the
foreground ... "I'm tired, relieved... don't give me no *kak* no more!"

the different characters had responded under what they believed was the 'real'
thing. I radioed back to Omauni using the HF set and the Buffels arrived a
little later. We bussed the bemused, relieved Signallers back to Omauni to have
a square meal and a good shower.

The signals training was done the following week in Omauni using an
Operational Signals Manual I had put together. It was a simple, practical
approach to signals using the bush techniques I had learned. Every afternoon
was spent on skill at arms and on the range. They got pretty accurate and
began to handle their weapons of choice, mainly standard issue R1s (FN) and
a few AK-47s, with a lot of confidence. With only three or four shots, they
began to make a tin can hop back over the sand wall we used as a range butt.

The final test for the course was splitting them up into teams of five, and
with their faces blacked out with 'black-is-beautiful' and blindfolded, we drove
them up to the Angolan border some 25km to the north. On debussing, the
blindfolds were removed, they were given a map and compass and told to

32 Battalion Signals Course, Final Selection - 2Lt MacMillan, 'miggie', net covering face, grenade and radio handset strapped on his chest.

32 Battalion Signals Course, Final Selection – The troops swapping war stories - Sergeant Gav Veenstra (top right) having a lot of fun hearing about their escapades.

make their way overnight back to a point a few kilometres out of the Omauni base. One of the teams radioed in with their HF set, informing us they had picked up some gook spoor and for a while we thought we might even bag a few 'kills' to round off the training, but the tracks turned out to be too old to pursue. That would have been one helluva thing … trainee Signallers with some real 'kills' to their name. I would either have been court-martialled or made a General on the spot!

On returning to the Battalion HQ at Rundu, those that we selected were awarded their coveted, camouflage 32 Battalion beret by Commandant Ferreira. They wore the standard Buffalo head badge on it with the Signals Corps colour flash beneath it. I selected a four-man Ops signals team who were the top guys. I chose Corporal John Bodley as the Ops team leader and he became the 2nd in command of the signals troop in the process. I had 'found' him some months back languishing in a logistics warehouse in Rundu, generally causing mayhem with his questioning attitude and irrepressible sense of humour. These were qualities I valued if channelled, so I had him transferred to the signals unit in Three-Two. He did well while I was there … if I ever find out he didn't continue to perform well after I left, I'll break his head.

They had hardly been on the Border three weeks and they had been pushed to their mental and physical limits whilst being introduced to the bush war. Having passed the Signals Selection, I was confident that should any of the Signallers find themselves in a situation such as I had found myself in at Savate, I had given them the tools they needed not only to survive, but to acquit themselves well. I could also see that it had given them a feeling of pride and a real sense of 'esprit de corps' to be a Signaller in Three-Two.

And if anyone ever called them 'Seiner' with that despised tone of disrespect, I hoped they would have what it took to tell them to fuck off… as they were now combat-trained 32 Battalion Signallers.

18
Selection course

The new infantry officers and NCOs were put through a selection course down at the Buffalo base. Having received excellent infantry training back in South Africa, the emphasis was on learning basic Portuguese and the ways of bush fighting used by the Battalion. Signals was part of it – I kept it simple and practical. We were downriver from the main base, and about 8km up from the Botswana border. Being alongside the Kavango River, it was a beautiful part of the country. With some large trees scattered throughout the floodplains on the eastern side of the river and with marshlands out to the west, it was a game reserve of sorts thanks to the tireless efforts of some of the Three-Two guys. As a result, the area boasted a herd of about 600 buffalo and the same number of elephant.

On the Saturday, the instructors got to have a *braai* (barbeque) while the guys on the selection course lived on their rat packs and slept in slit trenches out in the bush somewhere. After a few beers, someone decided it would be a good idea to go fishing. We loaded a case of hand grenades into a boat and headed out onto the river with the gunwales marginally above the waterline as no one wanted to stay behind. Any likely spot had a grenade thrown in it. We were not doing too good as we were down to two grenades and had nothing to show for it … much shouting, laughter and clearly too many chiefs and too few Indians around. We finally identified a good spot and one of the sergeants was selected to do the throwing. As the grenade arched high into the air, we realised it would land in only a few centimetres of water … and the mad scramble was suddenly on to be first to the bottom of the boat to avoid the shrapnel. It exploded only a few metres from us, showering us with water and mud. Luckily no one was hurt.

Slightly sobered, we headed upriver and carefully selected the final spot within which to use our one remaining grenade. It was perfect. The grenade exploded one metre below the surface of the water and about eight stunned fish floated belly-up. With a roar of excitement, all but one of us leapt into the crocodile infested waters to retrieve our prizes. Grabbing a fish, I stuck the tail in my mouth to grab another, when I noticed the boat floating off downriver

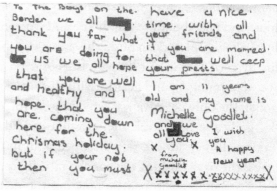

To The Boys on the Border we all ▉ thank you for what you are doing for ▉ us we all hope that you are well and healthy and I hope. that you are. coming down here for the. Chrismas holiday. but if your nob then you must have a nice. time. with all your friends and if you are marred. that ▉ well ceep your prests

I am 11 years old and my name is Michelle Goodlet. and ▉ we all ▉ love I wish you X you X A happy new year from michelle Goodlet

X X X X X X X·XXXX xxxxX

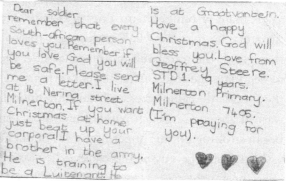

Dear soldier remember that every South-african person loves you. Remember if you love God you will be safe. Please send me a letter. I live at 16 Nerina street Milnerton. If you want Christmas at home just beat up your corporal I have a brother in the army. He is training to be a Luitenant. He is at Grootvanbein. Have a happy Christmas. God will bless you. Love from Geoffrey Steere. STD 1. 4 years. Milnerton Primary. Milnerton 7405. (I'm praying for you).

Two of the cards made by children back in South Africa
and sent up to us by the Southern Cross Fund.

with the strong current. The guy sitting alone in the boat was a rookie admin officer just up from the 'States', his face pale and his eyes wide as saucers. I abandoned the other fish and struck out for the boat, racing the other guys in the water. A good distance down we finally caught up with the boat and all piled in, panting somewhat, laughing and ribbing each other about who had swum fastest to get away from the crocs. We headed back for our fish *braai* with only about three fish to show for our efforts.

With the sun setting and the Kavango River quietly gurgling close by, we wrapped the fish in tinfoil, buried them a few centimetres beneath the sand and built a fire on top of them – boy, did they taste good a few hours later when we dug them out. Copious amounts of Castle Lager fuelled the usual animated conversations … war, home and women … and then we would change the topic and talk about the war, home and women … and so it went! Surrounded by the beautiful African bush, the stars close above us in the inky black sky, we finally curled up in our sleeping bags under a bush or somewhere in the open. We were young, fit and healthy with the rest of our lives ahead of us … life was good. The only negative was why we were there in the first place.

Early the next week the selection candidates were doing river crossings. Taking all their kit off, they wrapped it all in their ponchos and floated them across the river, pushing the poncho rafts in front of them as they swam behind. The instructors, who had by now been joined by the RSM, Sergeant Major Ueckerman, were in the aluminium assault boats (one of which we had used for our weekend's fishing trip). They were cruising around, tossing grenades into the water at regular intervals to keep the crocs at bay.

A mate of mine, Shaun Prior was with one of the 'sticks' of five. This is the story he told me when he finished the course a few weeks later. When they got to the reed bank on the other side, they put their kit on and started to negotiate the reeds. After initially struggling through the dense vegetation, they suddenly came across a beautiful, smooth, wide hippo path. Although warned about using such paths, they threw caution to the wind and happily began strolling up this 'super-highway'. Suddenly, there was a commotion and a shout from the guy at the back as he was tossed into the air by a buffalo charging up the path. The next guy got shouldered to the ground while the rest of them managed to throw themselves to one side as it thundered passed. Dusting themselves off, they were collecting themselves together when the second buffalo hit them. The guy at the back got tossed in the air again and it then went for the second guy still dazed on the ground from the first one, pinning him down with the boss of its horns. Struggling beneath the horns, he was screaming for his mates not to shoot as he was more scared of them killing him than he was about the buffalo doing him in. Shaun was barely three metres from the beast, and ignoring his friend's pleas, fired five rounds (all he was allowed to carry on selection course) at point blank range into the side of the buffalo. It staggered back, and rumbled off up the path towards the other one.

On hearing the commotion RSM Ueckerman stood up in his assault boat, filled his great chest and began bellowing over the radio (he may as well not of been using it he was shouting so loud) … "*Wat die fok gaan aan?*" ("What the fuck is going on?") On getting the story and realising a buffalo was wounded, he ordered them to hunt it down and destroy it. A wounded buffalo is undoubtedly the most dangerous animal in Africa. This was going to be no mean feat! We spent the rest of the day back in the Tac HQ alongside the river, plotting the progress of Shaun and his team on the map-board, as they called in their positions over the radio. I was amazed at their audacity and bravery in pursuing the buffalo through such inhospitable terrain … sodden read beds, dense bush, and swamps … you name it! Nothing held them back! This also impressed the hell out of the RSM, who, being very proud of his boys, called them off the hunt as the sun began to set. Misty eyed, he went on to tell them over the radio that it was the bravery and audacity they had showed that embodied the spirit of the Battalion and that it was endeavour such as theirs, that set our unit apart and made it the elite it was. It was quiet a stirring speech … it really drew me in and I also got a bit choked up!

I met up with Shaun Prior when they had completed the selection a few weeks later, and rushed over to shake his hand and congratulate him on his daring exploit. He roared with laughter, and taking me aside he quietly explained that they hadn't moved an inch the whole day, merely calling in fictitious positions as to where they should have been if they had in fact been hunting down the dreaded buffalo. Now *that* for me certainly embodied the audacity and approach of a Three-Two Battalion soldier! Live to fight another day was always top-of-mind, as was only standing to fight when you can do so on your own terms!

No surprise for me when the Battalion was awarded its colours on turning 10 years old in 1986, and at the same time, acknowledged as being the most successful South African Army fighting unit since the Second World War.

19
'Min' days and a sense of honour

My role in the training of the selection course was over a lot quicker than I had anticipated, and it gave me the opportunity to have two weeks of golden days in the Caprivi. Back in the main Buffalo base, I stayed with the Signallers in a bungalow vacated for my personal use. Set amongst tall trees and lush bush, it overlooked the Kavango River. Every evening we had a good few beers in the very smart Buffalo Base 'ladies bar' (only no ladies!) and then slept in late the following morning. We would get up just in time for brunch, which finished at 10am. Fortified with glorious bacon and eggs, and dressed in just a pair of shorts and takkies, we took an R1 rifle to guard against crocodiles and hippos and spent the day tiger fishing. We didn't catch anything but then again, that wasn't really the point. We would lie in the calf-deep water where it flowed over a sand bank, with the rifle held just above the water by two forked sticks ... not a cloud in the sky, not a breath of wind, with the emerald green water sliding by. Then we would organise a fire in the evenings amongst the tall trees, *braaing* steaks as we looked out over the beautiful river with its broad sand banks, vast reed beds and surrounding, lush green bush; and then beers in the 'ladies bar' again ... no matter how pissed we got, we never did get to find those ladies! After the beers, it was often a challenge to find our way through the bush to our bungalows, particularly as we had to be careful not to bump into any elephant, buffalo or hippo in our happily inebriated state.

The evenings not spent in the pub gave me time to spend alone, surrounded by the sounds of the African bush, looking out over the silvery reed beds and the dark majestic river. Sitting quietly outside my bungalow reminded me of my time at the beginning of the year, sitting outside the fishing shack opposite Dirico, looking at the same river, gazing up towards where Willem Ratte and his team were packing explosives under the bridge. Now down at Buffalo, I shared the same solitude, the same magic of the reed beds as I had way back then ... the reeds standing silvery still in the moonlight again, rustling gently when the breeze moved over them, as if it were a whisper. It seemed as if they were helping me finally find the answers I had been looking for ... about life,

KERSFEES *1979* X-MAS
GRENSDIENS BORDER DUTY
CAPRIVI
S. W. A.
SA LEER   SA ARMY

With gratitude for your excellent and determined service I wish you a merry Christmas and I trust that in the new year you will share in the peace and prosperity you are helping to establish for the Republic of South Africa.

Mag die vrede en vreugde van die Kersgety u bewus maak van die waarde van u diens sodat dit by u ook sal gaan om: "Vir jou, Suid-Afrika".

M.A. de M. Malan
M.A. de M. Malan: Genl
Hoof van die SA Weermag
Chief of the SA Defence Force

The Southern Cross Fund was a voluntary women's organisation providing moral support to the South African National Serviceman. Amongst other things, Christmas cards and gifts were sent up to us on the Angola/South West African border and then randomly handed out to the soldiers.

death, the war, Three-Two …

While many issues took a lot longer to come to terms with, the answer to the question of why we were fighting the war in Namibia and Angola had finally begun to emerge. As a Signals Officer I had largely spent my time in various Headquarters and Tactical HQs. This had exposed me to the comments of the brass when they were chatting amongst themselves … and from this I had come to realise that the strategy for the South African Army was simply to keep the war out of South Africa and away from its borders, and in doing so, to allow the political situation to resolve itself back home. Our activities in South West Africa (Namibia) and Angola now made sense to me. And while there were many uncertainties at the time as to the final outcome, given our military strategy, I was certainly very comfortable with the role I had played. I thought back to the *braais* at Nkongo at the beginning of the year, when we had enthusiastically debated the morality and strategies behind the war. Fuelled by copious amounts of Castle Lager and further energised by youth and innocence we argued long and hard. In particular, I thought of my friend Heinz Muller and his '*Ons moet net voort fok*' ("We must just fuck forward") strategy for winning the war. Even with the irony of his death at Savate and my having survived, I couldn't help thinking with a wry smile what he would have had to say about my newfound wisdom. It all seemed a lifetime ago.

And Three-Two? The mystique of the Battalion and its combat success was what initially attracted me to the unit … but I had come across a whole lot more. Amidst all the complexities of war and the politics behind it, I had discovered a sense of honour. The incredible military capability of the Battalion was only made possible by black and white soldiers working and fighting shoulder to shoulder. It was a beacon of what was fundamentally right in a time characterised by racial segregation and all the friction that ensued, the Battalion's credo made official with the Trooping of the Colours five years later giving credence to my internalised thoughts ... honesty, loyalty, justice. This mutual respect across the colour line was for me perhaps the most significant characteristic of Three-Two. When the shooting starts, it's not the colour of the man's skin next to you that counts, it's what he is capable of. And Three-Two is right up there with the best of the best.

I also came to accept what had puzzled me at first ... and that was the realization that I did not hate the enemy. Their political party was known as SWAPO with their military wing being PLAN (People's Liberation Army of Namibia). They were extremely brave men who were fighting for an honourable cause; that of the independence of their country. I figured they had to rank amongst the finest guerrilla fighters in the world with the effectiveness with which they applied the principles of guerrilla warfare. The courage they displayed with not letting up with their activities in the face of the effectiveness of our anti-guerrilla tactics was exemplary. Missions into South West Africa from their bases deep in Angola were almost suicidal; once they had set out on their mission on foot they had no resupply of food and ammunition, medical evacuation or air support. The terrain they operated in offered little cover in that they were easily spotted from the air, the only thing in their favour being the vastness of the area. If they hit contact with our troops they would briefly stand their ground then they would bombshell and run... and run... and if we caught up with them using vehicles, spotter aircraft and helicopter gunships they died. And yet they were still not deterred, even with the odds being stacked against them and they kept up their war of attrition. So, far from hating them I had a huge amount of respect for their commitment to the principle behind their cause. Nonetheless they were still the enemy and I had my loyalties to my own country, even as confusing as our cause was at the time.

However, be that as it may, that time at Buffalo gave me nearly ten, glorious days of '*balas bakking*' (sunning your nuts) ... time to think, time to relax, and time to have a '*jol*'. I had a lot of fun one day, scaring the shit out of the guys after a lazy morning's tiger fishing. Crossing the wide sand bank we had to pick our way carefully through the thick reed bed, never sure what we would find lurking there. I made sure I got a little ahead of them as we headed back towards the bungalows set deep in the thick bush overlooking the river. Being out of view and around a corner, I jumped off the path and burrowed myself under a matted bed of reeds. As the guys were almost on top of me, I heaved the reeds up with my shoulders, letting out a great bellow at the same time. They all let out ear splitting screams and started lashing at the reeds with their spindly fishing rods, valiantly fighting off the buffalo or hippo they thought was attacking them. I laughed even more when I saw their sheepish faces when I threw the reeds off, and had great fun ribbing them about their girlish screams and choice of deadly weapons. I had made sure the guy carrying the rifle was in on my lark or he could have seriously spoilt my day!

The only blot on that time was that we lost one of our black troops to a crocodile. This was a fact of life at Buffalo as the Battalion would usually lose at least three troops a year to these age-old reptiles. He was washing his clothes in the river and was then standing waist-deep, bathing in the water. The croc was so big he only had time to throw his hands in the air and take a deep breath, before disappearing in front of his young son who was standing on the bank. We heard the commotion from our fishing spot farther down the river, and grabbing some hand grenades and jumping into an aluminium assault boat, we roared around tossing grenades into likely spots. We were hoping the croc would let him go, but by now he was more than likely dead. It proved a frustrating, fruitless exercise that left us sombre and introspective. We had been swimming in that very channel a few days previously.

I knew I could only stay under the radar for a limited period of time before having to get back to the Battalion HQ. After a week, signals started to arrive from HQ back in Rundu, questioning my whereabouts. I hitched a lift in a convoy and rode on the back of one of the big, open, Kwevoël lorries. For the first time I got covered in dust as my mates in the platoons had when they had been trooped anywhere. I soon curled myself into a ball on top of the cargo that was loaded on the flatbed, and cocooned myself in my thoughts, while the sun and the wind hammered me in a swirling cloud of dust for hour after jolting hour. I had certainly got used to the cool helicopter rides with the OC and the HQ group!

On getting back to Rundu and the Battalion HQ, the OC was very keen that I sign on for an extra year, or 'short service' as it was called. It was a difficult decision to make in the face of having been promoted to full Lieutenant and having been awarded the 32 Battalion Prestige Shield, which was an annual award for the most outstanding junior officer in the Battalion. I had also been cited for the Chief of SADF Commendation Medal for meritorious service (which came through the following year). But I felt I had given it my all and I was looking forward to getting back to civvy street, getting my degree from university, a girlfriend, a home, starting a family … essentially getting on with the life I had fought for.

Thus it was with very, very mixed feelings that I left 32 Battalion and Rundu just before Christmas of 1980. It was particularly difficult to hand in my R1 Assault Rifle. It had seldom left my side and had never let me down.

Rather than fly back home in the Flossie, I had got a lift with Willem Ratte in his little Nissan *bakkie*. With his arm still adorned with the gut-wrenching pins that stuck out of his arm all over the place, there to heal the wound he had suffered on Ops Chaka a few months previously, we drove from Rundu down through Namibia and all the way to Cape Town. I hadn't seen any of Namibia except for the Operational Area in the north, and enjoyed the vast open spaces and endless skies. I spent a lot of the time staring into the middle distance, beginning the process of trying to close my mind to the experiences of the past year. We didn't say much during the two-day drive. We didn't have to.

I said a quiet goodbye to Willem at the civilian airport and caught a flight back home to Durban.

20

Civvy street

I bought a brand new Alfa Romeo with the 'danger money' I had earned up on the border and spent a few months surfing before going to university. My girlfriend had waited for me during my National Service and so we began pretty much where we had left off fourteen months ago, the difference being that I had to get her to adjust to who I really was and not the image she had created in her mind when I was away.

I never really adjusted to life at university. My outlook on life had changed forever ... and as has been said, 'the first casualty of war is innocence'. I was outside looking in – something was missing for me ... a sense of pride, an 'espirit de corps', a real purpose to life? Everyone in civvy street was out for themselves; no-one could relate to my experiences and no one cared. Why should they anyway? They were strangely fascinated but would rather not know. It left me wondering if I had an emotional imbalance ... was something wrong with me, was I overreacting? I did some army 'camps' with 2 Reconnaissance Regiment during my university vacations, hoping for a balance. But it only served to illustrate the divide.

I found being back in South Africa and living in the midst of the policy of Apartheid confusing. After being in Three-Two where we had fought a war with such pride and with no racial segregation, something didn't make sense. I tried to ignore the madness around me and to get on with my life, trusting in God, and trusting in fate.

Although it will always be there with me, it took about ten years to constructively start putting it all behind me, to begin finding the perspective, to be able to think or talk about the Border War without an unsettling emotional pull settling in my stomach for a few hours. I suppose the passage of time played a role, but so did hunting. Initially I couldn't get myself to raise a rifle or shotgun, but I slowly came back round to facing it. Never enjoying it, it did however give me the means to face killing and to accept the hunter instinct built into us all. The preparation, the focus, the sense of purpose, the pursuit of 'one shot, one kill', the responsibility and implications of taking a life ... the lingering afterthoughts.

Those who didn't make it will remain with me forever. I think often of my friends Tim Patrick and Heinz Muller. Tim's memory carries an overbearing aura of youthful innocence and a life cut short before its time. The tragedy of his death in the pitched battle that was Savate, when he was still so young and for which he was so ill prepared, has weighed heavily on me over the years. The courage he displayed in throwing himself into the assault with Alpha Company when they knew they were heavily outnumbered is the only consolation I carry with me.

And it's always with the ghost of a smile that I think of Heinz and the fun we had sitting round campfires in the middle of the bush. Our raucous, beer-induced discussions on how best to fight the war… with the joviality and laughter increasing as we consumed ever more beer and our solutions to the world's problems became ever grander and grander as the fire died down, and the moon rose steadily above us. Heinz was the epitome of an infantry officer, strong and fit with an air of measured aggression about him. The irony for me has always been that I survived Savate and he didn't. His last words to me, *"Justin ! … . jy moet lekker wees"* ("Justin! …. you must be good"), have haunted me ever since. It was his way of saying goodbye, his way of telling me to get on with my life, to be strong, to be happy.

In times of hardship Heinz's words have always served as a source of inspiration. I like to think that I have lived up to his expectations.

21

The end ... the beginning

Three-Two continued to grow from strength to strength after my time. South Africa pushed a 50km no-go zone into Southern Angola in the early eighties and occupied the town of Ongiva. Three-Two had a permanent Tactical HQ there which I visited whilst on a 'camp' with 5 Recce. We came into Ongiva from Ondangwa on a Puma helicopter to refuel, before heading a couple of hundred kilometres north to drop off a reconnaissance 'stick'. It was a weird feeling sitting in the door of the chopper looking down at the town ... in 1980 we had always given it a wide birth as it was heavily fortified by the enemy.

By the mid 1980s Three-Two became a very different Battalion in order to more effectively support UNITA. Our resounding success at Savate, and countless other battles and skirmishes, seemed to have given the unit a sinister reputation, lending credence to the Angolan Army referring to us as 'Os Terreveis' ... 'The Terrible Ones'. Victory at Savate had led to the fall of all the FAPLA garrisons in south-eastern Angola and led to UNITA effectively controlling this vast area. By the mid 1980s, UNITA's successes merely served to escalate the conflict from a low-level counter-insurgency to a full-scale conventional war that threatened to spiral out of control. With the backing of the USSR and the active participation of the Cubans, the Angolan army from 1986 began a series of conventional attacks on the UNITA-controlled south-eastern corner of Angola. South Africa found itself increasingly drawn into kinetic war fighting in order to prevent UNITA being overrun. This resulted in fully conventional brigade-level actions in the late eighties at Quito Canavale and Mavinga, and the areas that surrounded them.

By then, Three-Two was equipped with Ratel armoured vehicles and had mobile multiple rocket systems, anti-aircraft guns and Ratel ZT3 anti-tank missile launchers assigned to them. They were also supported by G5 and G6 heavy artillery units, a far cry from the basic infantry weapons we had at Savate. Even in the big conventional battles that Three-Two fought towards the end of the Angola-Namibia conflict, it was interesting for me to note that in 1980 the battalion took more casualties than at any other time and in any other year.

However, the South African generals were alarmed with the increasing tempo of operations; the fighting had escalated way above their initial expectations. We seem to have only been 'saved by the bell' as it were, by the collapse of the USSR which led to their withdrawal of military support to the Cubans, which in turn made it increasingly difficult for the Cubans to continue aiding the Angolans. As neither Cuba, Angola, nor South Africa could afford to continue to fight a war on this scale, it provided the opportunity for a negotiated cease fire and a withdrawal of South African and Cuban forces from Angola. Without the unforeseen collapse of the Russian Empire, we may well have been fighting the communist-backed hordes from the very borders of South Africa, as opposed to keeping the war on the border of Angola and South West Africa (Namibia).

The withdrawal of the South Africans from Angola in 1988 and the negotiated ceasefire with Cuba, MPLA, UNITA and SWAPO, led directly to South West Africa gaining its independence in 1990 and its emergence as Namibia. The domino effect saw the unthinkable begin, unfolding in South Africa with Nelson Mandela, the leader of the ANC black resistance movement, being released from prison by the visionary nationalist leader President F.W. de Klerk. Seen by many of the right-wing Afrikaners as a traitor, and with the communist-backed freedom movements clamoring for revolutionary socialism on the left, it was a courageous path to follow. And so the process of the unimaginable began ... that of a negotiated constitution that entrenched an individual's rights and those of minority racial groups, and one that would ultimately lead to the first truly democratic elections in South Africa in 1994 ... one-man-one-vote, and black majority rule without the mayhem and economic collapse that seemed to characterise most other African countries. The apocalypse that had loomed before us while we were growing up as teenagers had been averted.

Upon independence, all South African troops were withdrawn from Namibia and Three-Two was relocated from Rundu, to an abandoned mining town in the Northwestern Cape, Pomfret. From this base they were used to police some of the townships surrounding South African cities, controlling the volatility leading up to the elections in 1994. It was a time that our country was on a knife-edge and the watching world held its breath. Unfortunately, Three-Two would appear to have been overly successful in keeping the peace. The new order appeared to consider it a mercenary force that was too dangerous to be left intact. The negotiated settlement included the disbandment of the

Savate Day Memorial Service, Zeerust, 2008: Lt Taylor
and Lieutenant-Colonel Willem Ratte.

Battalion. The troops had the option of either being integrated into other regular Army units, or to accept early retirement.

I had since got my Private Pilot's Licence and had a lot of fun flying a little Cessna 140 out there. Being before the days of GPS systems (or maybe I couldn't afford the early ones) I set off across the featureless North-Western Cape on a compass bearing. Brisk crosswinds blew me off course and I soon had a very tight fuel situation on my hands. Luck had it that I spotted the little pimple of a hill that marked Pomfret ... and if it hadn't been the one, I would have had to do a precautionary landing in the bush. But then again, I had my old Three-Two kit in the back so I guess I would have been ok.

The final parade was held that afternoon. Charged with emotion it was incredible watching those battle-hardened troops standing so proud. Those of us of the old guard stood to one side, each cocooned in our own thoughts and emotions, and as a group, spanning the full history of the Battalion. Then the parade was over, and they marched off, wheeling across the parade ground, platoon after platoon, company after company. They sang their battle songs with unflinching pride, in perfect unison to the thump of their boots,

Savate Day Memorial Service, Zeerust, 2008: Lt Justin Taylor with
the legendary Colonel Jan Breytenbach (who founded 32 Battalion)
and Corporal Peter Lipman (Savate vet) on the right.

the heartrending, throaty roar of well over a thousand veterans of countless
skirmishes, countless battles. They fittingly marched west towards Angola and
Namibia, into the setting sun with the ochre red dust of the Kalahari swirling
up amongst their ranks.

I stood quietly squinting in the direction they had marched … completely
lost in my thoughts and with my emotions threatening to overwhelm me. I
noticed two young black boys leading a tall, lean, black 32 Battalion soldier by
the hand in the direction the rest of them had gone. With a brace of medals
on his chest and his camouflage beret placed perfectly on his head, he walked
proudly with his back straight, his shoulders squared and his chin up.

He was blind.

22

The miracle that was

Thirty-two years later, to the day ... 21 May 2012, I stood on the battlefield again at Savate in Angola. And at exactly the same time the battle begun ... 9.00am Angolan time, wearing our now faded berets and formed up as a squad, we saluted the memorial we had just erected.

It was truly remarkable that we were back. Standing there at attention with my eyes fixed on the memorial, I suddenly felt a huge sense of release. Looking up at the slope above us where hidden amongst the trees, the trenches were still marked in the sand and battle debris still lay scattered around, the images and sounds of that vicious action came back to me as if it were only yesterday. On that day we had been intent on killing each other, and doing a pretty good job of it too. Here we were, now at peace, putting it all behind us with a surreal feeling of goodwill and mutual respect.

My thoughts went back to a time when we were facing an apocalypse whichever way we turned. In its attempt to avoid the chaos that had enveloped most of the rest of Africa, the discriminatory policy of Apartheid had offered the promise of civil war and bloodshed with the added threat of the neighbouring frontline states boiling over our borders in their support. And the alternative at the time, that of capitulating to one-man-one-vote with its threat of black communist rule, nationalisation and economic collapse was unthinkable. And neither had happened. The unimaginable had played itself out.

The collapse of the Russian Empire with its threat of global communist domination in the mid-eighties had allowed us the opportunity to negotiate our withdrawal from Angola and this had resulted in the independence of South West Africa; Namibia. And the most unthinkable of them all ... democratic elections in South Africa in 1994, one-man-one-vote, black majority rule ... without the mayhem we feared that had characterised other African states. The new South Africa had been born, and with it the promise of a future for us all, working together regardless of race or religion. And while there were those that felt betrayed by it all, it was the only way forward even though there is always the chance that it will all unravel. So far the new era has stood the test of time. With the nightmare our country faced in the seventies and eighties,

Savate Day Memorial Service, Savate, 21 May 2012: Final touches
to the memorial erected in Savate village square.

Savate, 21 May 2012: thirty-two years to the day that the battle
began – unexploded ordnance still lying on the battlefield.

Savate, 21 May 2012: thirty-two years to the day that the battle began. The airfield in the middle of the Savate army base. Originally built by the Portuguese prior to 1975, it was bombed in the mid-1980s to render it inoperable. Below is one of several bomb craters.

the fact that it has been a peaceful transition and stable democracy with our constitution intact is a miracle ... an incredible example of tolerance and reconciliation in the face of the unthinkable, an inspiration for all mankind.

Three-Two seemed to me to symbolise the miracle we had lived through in Southern Africa over the previous thirty-two years. Having been an integral part of the process, the unit seemed to reflect the new at a time when we were mired in the old, and while it had had its share of controversy, Three-Two offered an example of what was right, as opposed to what was wrong... a sense of honour, a sense of integrity. As the Battalion faded away with its disbandment, the baton seemed to have been taken up by the entire country with the ushering in of a new era ... that of a non-racial South Africa and Nelson Mandela's Rainbow Nation.

And now here we were having been welcomed back by the Angolans and unbelievably, back at Savate ... not only at peace, but with a strong and mutual feeling of goodwill and respect, of bygones being bygones and of looking to the future with a keen sense of anticipation.

Turning my gaze away from the slope upon which we had fought so hard and on which so many had died, I fixed my eyes on the granite memorial again ... and found the closure I had been seeking for all of these 32 years. My friends Tim Patrick and Heinz Muller's names were up there with the rest of them. I thought of the last time I saw Tim, his youthful face with that preoccupied, detached look in his eyes and his brave smile. And I could see myself sitting around a campfire with Heinz again, beers in hand and us laughing together at our differences of opinion as to how to fight the war, and being young, fit and living our adventure. The inspiration I have drawn from them is that life has little to do with dying young and everything to do with living young ... live your adventure every day. I thought again of Heinz's last words to me which had been "Justin ... *jy moet lekker wees!*" ("Justin ... you must go well"). Now it was my turn and I quietly said to myself ... "*Julle moet lekker wees*" ... *you both* must go well" ...

It was done.

Savate no longer represented conflict and grief but was now a symbol of reconciliation, hope, pride and integrity. While defeated at Savate, the Angolan army had proved to be a worthy adversary and they could also stand tall and with their heads held high. I felt humbled to have fought shoulder to shoulder here at the Battle of Savate with the troops of 32 Battalion – I would not have wanted any other soldiers at my side. With its outstanding combat record and racial integration ahead of its time, I am honoured to have served with this unique battalion. While Three-Two may be no longer, it is a unit that is so unique, its spirit will forever be out there in the savannahs and forests of Africa.

On sun-filled days and beautiful starlit nights across Africa, the whisper in the reeds will, for me, forever carry the story of Three-Two.

The war is over for me now, but it will always be there for the rest of my days … but be that as it may, those of us who did make it have an obligation to build again, to teach to others what we know, and to try with what's left of our lives to find a goodness and meaning to this life.

Charlie Sheen as 'Taylor', *Platoon*, MGM 1987

Appendix

Poems

Battle of Savate
21 May 1980

Fear,
Subdued by the magnitude
Of aggressive events,
Developing level-headed mechanisms
Desperate survival.

Despair,
Sinking into a chasm
Borne of friends suddenly no more,
Becoming an animal's indifference to killing.

Caught in a void,
Walls of unleashed destruction
Cemented by the roar of vices,
Death ... the opening of a window.

Mindless helplessness,
A nothing...
Enveloped in winds of fear,
Values and morals of shifting dunes.

Relief,
Pathetic in its intensity
Familiar faces –
Bastions of trailing lifelines... shreds of hope.

Drained,
Vacuums of the aftermath,
New lights of oppressive realities
... shadows.

28 January 1981

My War
1980

Oppressive subjectiveness
... stretching

Heavy thoughts,
Low and swollen.
Sinister mists.
Obscurity.

Objective reality
Crushing all sweetness of past treasures,
Darkening the hopes and dreams
Of youth.

Slipping,
Grasping at suggestions of truth
In the belief of societies morals,
Values...
Shaken foundations.

Becoming helpless aggression,
Anchored,
For fear of being forgotten,
... despair.

15 March 1981

"The purpose of war is to serve a political end, but the true nature of war is to serve itself."

von Clausewitz

Related titles published by Helion & Company and GG Books

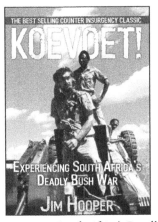

Koevoet! Experiencing South Africa's Deadly Bush War
Jim Hooper
312pp Paperback
ISBN 978-0-957058-70-6

LZ Hot! Flying South Africa's Border War
Nick Lithgow
174pp Paperback
ISBN 978-1-908916-59-4

*Three Sips of Gin. Dominating the Battlespace
with Rhodesia's Elite Selous Scouts*
Timothy Bax
448pp Paperback
ISBN 978-1-909384-29-3

HELION & COMPANY
26 Willow Road, Solihull, West Midlands B91 1UE, England
Telephone 0121 705 3393   Fax 0121 711 4075
Website: http://www.helion.co.uk

Lightning Source UK Ltd.
Milton Keynes UK
UKOW06f1300150216

268393UK00004B/24/P